Good House Cheap House

KIRA OBOLENSKY

Good House

Adventures in Creating
an Extraordinary Home
at an Ordinary Price

Photographs by Randy O'Rourke

Cheap House

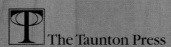
The Taunton Press

The Taunton Press
Inspiration for hands-on living®

The Taunton Press, Inc., 63 South Main Street,
PO Box 5506, Newtown, CT 06470-5506
e-mail: tp@taunton.com

Editor: Erica Sanders-Foege
Jacket/Cover design: Alexander Isley, Inc.
Interior design/Layout: Jeannet Leendertse
Photographer: Randy O'Rourke

LIBRARY OF CONGRESS CATALOGING-IN-PUBLICATION DATA
Obolensky, Kira.
  Good house cheap house / Kira Obolensky ; photographer: Randy O'Rourke.
     p. cm.
  ISBN 1-56158-752-4
  1. Dwellings--Design and construction. I. O'Rourke, Randy. II. Title.

  TH4811.O26 2005
  690'.837--dc22

                    2005001439

The following manufacturers/names appearing in *Good House Cheap House* are trademarks:
ApplePly®, Blu Dot®, Corian®, Dumpster®, eBay®, Flatpak®, Formica®, Galvalume®,
Hardipanel®, Hardiplank®, IKEA®, Jacuzzi®, Kalwall®, Lego®, Lincoln Logs®, Lithochrome®,
Parallam®, Richlite®, Sheetrock®, Simpson Strong-Tie®, Sonotube®

Acknowledgments

This book was really born from comments I received from a group of smart, budget-conscious friends who have enjoyed other books I've written but who were aware they were priced out of most of the featured projects. I want to thank them for suggesting that a book about unique houses they could actually afford would be of interest. I agree—and I'm grateful that The Taunton Press did as well.

There are lots of people to acknowledge and to thank. First and foremost would be the many people who helped me find the architects and houses featured here. Those include Stephen Sharpe at Texas AIA; Marianne Filloux in Bozeman, Montana; Brenda Taylor at the AIA offices in Wisconsin; Camille LeFevre at Minnesota AIA; and fellow Taunton authors Caren Connolly and Louis Wasserman.

I so enjoyed meeting homeowners and architects during the research part of the book, and my thanks extend to all who so graciously showed me their handiwork, fed me, and regaled me with tales and tips. Special thanks to my husband and family for baby-sitting, while I was enjoying myself in other parts of the country—and for their ideas and excitement about this topic.

I had some great conversations along the way, a few of which I want to acknowledge: Gail Peter Gordon in North Carolina about suburbs; Gar Hargens of Close Associates and Mary Fitch of Washington, D.C., AIA about homeowner choice; John DeForest about value; Carson Looney about design basics; and Tom Sternal and Geoff Warner about prefab.

This book was really shaped and affected by the people who work at The Taunton Press: Maureen Graney, Maria Taylor, and my editor, Erica Sanders-Foege, were integral to both its conception and execution. My sincere thanks for all their questions, suggestions, and collective intelligence. Thanks also to Katie Solomonson for her feedback and to Tom and Laura DeBiaso for their help with a last-minute author photo. Finally, I want to thank the photographer, Randy O'Rourke, whose images grace the pages of this book; I am grateful for his talents.

Contents

Introduction

I don't spend much time dreaming about a country estate or a marble bathroom. I'm a child of the D.I.Y. movement, steeped in "How-To" TV and books. I'm firmly locked in the group demographers call "cultural creatives," and my dream house is different. It will leave money in the bank for an interesting daily life and a vacation or two—and I'm willing to roll up my sleeves and work to get it.

An architect friend of mine has built an entire career out of working with people like me. His clients' budgets have inspired him to create his own style—marked by an inventive and playful use of inexpensive materials. We worked with him about seven years ago to renovate our kitchen in an Arts and Crafts style house.

We started our design process by listing the things we thought we wanted and then we compromised. A tile backsplash turned into a slate backsplash when we discovered acres of recycled chalkboards. The sink of our dreams cost an alarming $800. I found the exact sink, slightly used, with a fancy German faucet at a local recycling center. Cost? $50. I felt like I'd just won the jackpot. Instead of granite countertops, we opted for Formica®, but we had them finished with a thick aluminum edge that gives the kitchen an old-fashioned feeling. We stripped linoleum off the floors (ourselves) and had the original wooden floors underneath sanded, stained, and finished. We decided to try to use as many of the existing cabinets as possible.

Our splurge was a skylight, which transforms the space with light. Because the area is relatively small and the skylight is big, the architect created a sculptural frame made of Baltic birch plywood, which helps integrate the skylight into the ceiling. And we didn't compromise on handcrafted leather pulls on the drawers. Filled with the warmth of old wood and new light, our kitchen is now a beautiful, welcoming space. It's amazing, but we kept to our modest budget.

I am consistently more excited by a resourceful approach to space than by the most expensive, fully loaded luxury homes. I'm a ripper, at least when it comes to magazines, and when I look at what I've collected in my "dream house folder," I see small, funky, interesting, unique homes and rooms, all of which are budget beauties. This might say something about the size of my dreams, but it also acknowledges that good design can happen even when there's no money for extravagance.

This book puts forth an alternative to the many books that are about good expensive houses. It proves that you don't have to be a millionaire to live in a home that is special. The houses shown within all express an extraordinary spirit, which has been imbued by the people who have created them. I hope they will prove inspirational to you.

—*Kira Obolensky*

A House
within Reach

I f necessity is the mother of invention, then a budget is the muse of the good, cheap house. The good, or well-designed, house is easy to spot: It's got dynamic form; nicely proportioned and practical interior space; pleasing detailing; and a lasting quality. A good, cheap house is no exception—it just costs less. But there's more to getting a good, cheap house than spending less money. Merely cheap houses are readily available in the form of tract homes that seem to crop up overnight. In this book, the *good,* cheap house distinguishes itself from just cheap through design, experimentation, and ingenuity, all of which can transform an inexpensive structure into one that has value and worth.

1 This renovation of a nineteenth-century carriage house used the strategy of retaining not replacing: The timbers in this former hayloft were revealed during the construction, as was the floor, which is the back side of old bead board.

2 There's no one aesthetic at work in a good, cheap house. This contemporary home in Austin, Texas, combines loft-like interiors with a spare modern exterior.

1 Living large in a gem of a home. Built for $70,000, this house achieves its low cost by staying small. An outdoor room is protected by plantings and by the galvanized metal, which makes an L-shaped wall that partially encloses it.

These days, it seems that good design is a mainstream commodity. Savvy, design-conscious consumers buy attractive clothing hampers, coffee makers, and even computers because they want good-looking products for the right price.

For those who understand good design, a house that is affordable and unique is much harder to find—the marketplace doesn't readily offer affordable architecture. Although this concept has yet to find a mainstream venue, architects who are reading the trends are beginning to address this growing demand. And adventuresome homeowners with real budgets—whether they're first timers or retirees—are making their way into this territory with a willingness to do what it takes to get a good house for less.

Affordable, but better

Unfortunately, the term *affordable housing* brings to mind a grim image of what has traditionally constituted low-income housing in this country. Given the chance, a few of the homes featured in this book could really change what most low-income housing looks like. But many of the houses here cost, when you figure in extra design fees and inflation, a little more than a typical builder house (yet a whole lot less than a house featured in most design magazines).

The cheapest house featured here was built in Maine on an assembly line, and it would cost about $68/sq. ft. if built today. The most expensive, at $185/sq. ft., was completed a couple of years ago on an island off of Seattle. Bear in mind that building costs vary widely from region to region, as does the cost of land. (The prices quoted throughout this book are generally for construction only.) The architect's fee, which is usually 10 percent to 15 percent of the construction cost, can also vary, depending on the extent of the services provided. For example, a house that costs $75/sq. ft. to build, would, if you included that fee, be closer to $82 to $85. For those houses that are not brand new, there's inflation to factor in at about 5 percent per year—so what cost $50/sq. ft. in the early 1990s, would be closer to $90/sq. ft. today, in 2005.

The good, cheap house does not rely solely on cost per square foot as a barometer of affordability. Sometimes, the square footage price is higher, because the bulk of the budget was spent on design, materials, or creating the space

2 It doesn't look modular, because it's designed by an architect. Basic design concepts at work here include balanced proportion, plenty of light, and a clear focal point (the wood-stove) in the living room.

3 The bungalow, which entered the American domestic landscape about 100 years ago, was a house designed and built for the middle class. It combined quality with affordability.

2

itself. The 352-sq.-ft. gem on the Puget Sound shown above was built for $70,000. By streamlining the interior spaces and creating an open connection to the outdoors, the architects designed a cabin that works so well its owner now lives there year round.

The good, cheap house of the past

The concept of good and cheap isn't a new one. The bungalow and Frank Lloyd Wright's post-Depression, futuristic Usonian houses are good reminders of how both developers and designers have attempted to address the needs of people on a budget. About 100 years ago, the bungalow was a cheaper, smaller version of what more wealthy people were building. It offered an efficient floor plan, which often included a fireplace, built-in furniture, and a front porch.

The Usonian house, on the other hand, was an attempt

3

1 The homeowners who built this masonry house in Wisconsin burned down the existing house on the lot—with the help of their local fire department—to save on demolition costs.

2 When Frank Lloyd Wright conceived of his Usonian houses, he may as well have designed this cheap, chic cabin in New Hampshire. The materials are industrial and the design is deceptively simple.

to redefine residential architecture. Making generous use of concrete and plywood, it introduced new building methods in an attempt to bring high design to the middle class at a low cost.

Good, cheap today

These days, there are common denominators that factor into making a good, cheap house, which the stories in this book illuminate. The homeowner in search of good *and* cheap has to be open to adventure and to new ideas and be willing to participate in the design and building process. Design is a big part of the equation because, in most instances, using an architect is what has transformed a house from one that is cheap to one that is unique. And finally, these houses are composed of inexpensive materials used in innovative ways, inspired by thrift, a desire for quality, and a playful approach to home design.

The adventure quotient What's become clear in writing this book is that behind every good, cheap house is a story.

3 Located an hour outside of the Twin Cities, this modern interpretation of a rural structure is a paragon of the D.I.Y. mentality. Not only did its owners participate in the building process but so did the architects, who run an innovative firm that both designs and builds projects.

These homeowners have literally gone the extra mile to get something special. They've driven across state lines to find good prices on materials, "baked" copper fixtures in their home ovens to create brown patina, beautified concrete sub-flooring with stain, and plastered their own walls. Some have even had local firefighters use the dilapidated homes on their lots as training facilities to save on demolition costs.

One Minnesota couple was dead set on getting prized materials for their home. They ripped out and hauled 5,000 linear ft. of recycled wood themselves from a falling-down farmhouse. They trained students from the local high school to help dry-stack stone over a 6-month period, and they went Dumpster®-diving for 30 recycled windows. These homeowners were tenacious and savvy; and, in the end, the house they created (*above*) is one that could easily grace the pages of a high-end design publication.

Other adventures represent a wide range, from how to use industrial bridge washers as decorative detail to sheathing a garden-variety refrigerator in stainless steel to transforming irrigation pipes into columns for a portico. What becomes clear is that making a house on any kind of budget is a monumental process, filled with imagination and resourcefulness.

The design factor In many instances, the most important choice these homeowners made was finding the right architect and builder. Many wisely brought a builder in during the design process or worked with a design/build firm. An architect may be willing to take on a good, cheap house when a client is motivated and open to new ideas. Often, architects just starting out are looking to expand their design portfolios. Some feel obligated to make their work available to people who may not otherwise be able to afford it. Still others who are more established may take on this type of challenge because it offers a welcome change from the higher-end work they usually do.

Another group of architects are eliminating the traditional relationship with a contractor altogether by using prefab building methods. Although much new housing in this country is prefabricated or manufactured (meaning it's built off-site and then delivered in components), the prefab homes shown here are more expensive because they incorporate design. Architect-designed prefab houses combine the expenses saved in construction with design to create good value.

Charlie Lazor, the architect who designed the Flatpak® house (at left) has another description for these homes: *manufactured architecture*. For him, architecture belongs in

1. The Flatpak house system comes in shrink-wrapped panels and is put together on-site. This prototype, designed by a founder of Blu Dot® furniture, signals the coming arrival of good home design in the main-stream marketplace.

2. This suburban home was built for $150,000 outside of Bozeman, Montana. It's a striking standout that also manages to be respectful of its more traditional neighbors.

the marketplace alongside the other commodities that combine affordability with design.

These architect-designed prefab homes are on the cutting edge of what I hope will eventually be more widely available. In the meantime, there are plenty of houses here that were traditionally built, well designed, and affordable. For example, a house in Bozeman, Montana, cost under $150,000 to build. It was designed by an architect for a couple who couldn't afford rising rents. It's beautifully sited, and the rooms are generously proportioned and filled with creative detail. Clad in cement-board lap siding with an unusual picture window made from skylight material, it sits in a suburban enclave and shares the same views of the mountains as the nearby high-end McMansions and vinyl-clad ramblers.

It's a material world Home-improvement stores have proved to be a rich source for anyone wanting to build inexpensively. Concrete, cement fiberboard, plywood, and glass are generally associated with industrial contexts; but, as you'll see, residential architects and homeowners are incorporating these low-cost, high-quality products into their designs. For example, galvanized corrugated metal, long used for barn roofs, makes for practical and funky cladding on an otherwise traditional house. Less-expensive hardwood veneer plywood can evoke the same feeling as solid wood. Cement board can be made to look like wood, oxidized steel, corrugated metal, or dressed up with an aluminum reveal.

Other items are applied in unexpected ways—patio doors are used as windows, sand-blasted acrylic is made into doors, and galvanized metal lines a shower stall. In the hands of a pro, stock items can be readily transformed into something that looks a lot more expensive. After all, good design is, well, good design. A house in North Carolina uses wood siding on the floors, plywood on the walls, and steel cable on the stairs. Here, materials that are in and of themselves less expensive create spaces that are just as distinctive as those filled with hardwood, marble, and stone.

Secrets of good and cheap revealed

The budgets in this book run the gamut from shoestring to modest, but all of them have allowed the homeowners to take

resourceful, creative approaches to space. A $30,000 budget transformed a squalid Washington, D.C., row house into a stylish home. A log cabin in Bozeman, Montana, was renovated into a contemporary pad for $50,000; a spec house in Austin, Texas, designed and built by one forward-thinking architecture firm, sold in 2004 for $180,000, including the land. As you read on, I think you'll find that the stories these houses tell are as inspirational as their affordable prices.

About half of the houses in this book were built by architects for themselves. As professionals, naturally these architects have an advantage. For them, their homes are deeply personal statements. Their willingness to experiment is key to the places they build. As a result, theirs represent some of the best of what good, cheap houses can be.

The rest of the homes in this book were built by and for people at virtually every stage of life. All of them had real budgets but wanted more design than what developers were building or what was already on the market.

The 27 houses in this book prove that with ingenuity, planning, sweat equity, the skills of a good designer, and a sense of adventure, you can live in a unique home that you can actually afford.

3   This sophisticated house in the Pacific Northwest combines inexpensive materials with higher-end finishes. The cladding is Hardipanel®, but the inset aluminum reveals required precision and more expensive carpentry skills.

4   Low-cost materials from a home-improvement store have been transformed through good design into artful architecture in this North Carolina residence.

Portfolios

Columns

The front columns on this house in an Albuquerque subdivision are not remotely Greek, Arts and Crafts, or Victorian in style. They are, in fact, made from the same corrugated metal pipe used in drainage ditches throughout New Mexico. The columns don't pretend to be anything than what they are, and this seems to be the key to the good design this house exudes: Inexpensive materials are used honestly, replacing high-end alternatives both inside and outside the house.

Architect Lee Gamelsky first started working with the homeowners in 1996: the husband was just out of medical school and their building budget was a firm $75/sq. ft. The couple wanted each room in the house to get light from two exposures, so Lee decided on a linear plan, meaning that each room would lead directly to another. The couple was also looking for something that was different from the typical suburban houses found in this area, which tended toward overscale "puebloids," as one local describes them.

Built by a young couple with a budget of $75/sq. ft., this house employs inexpensive materials in a straightforward way. The front columns are made from corrugated galvanized pipes typically used in drainage ditches.

1

There's a strong connection to the outdoors in this house, with its porches, loggias, and patios. The glass blocks that punctuate the long expanse of stucco add light while filtering the strong western sun.

Inside, the glass blocks create a distinctive pattern in the hallway. Further light is provided by sconces, which were made by a sheet-metal shop out of copper.

The house, which was recently sold to a retired couple, presents a modest stucco face—with its metal roof and vinyl windows—to the street. There's a courtyard visible through the front entrance, but little to indicate on the outside the kind of rustic simplicity featured inside. Not pretentious or even attention getting, the home manages to be the most interesting one in the subdivision.

Unique places within
The horseshoe configuration creates an interior courtyard and allows plenty of sunlight. Bedrooms are on one wing; guest bedroom/office, kitchen, and family room are on the other wing. In the middle sits a central living room, the focal point of the home.

This striking central space is welcoming and filled with "industrial" details. What looks like Italian terracotta tile on the floor is really poured concrete, diamond-saw cut in a pattern and grouted, then finished by the original owners with a Scoffield Lithochrome® stain, and finally sealed.

The fireplace mantel is made from a steel I-beam and decorated with 3-in. bridge washers, the 16-ft. vaulted ceiling is covered in fir, and the beams are supported with structural steel angle iron. The old-style sconce lighting was fashioned by a metal shop from sheet copper that the couple "baked" in their oven to create the brown patina.

Each space feels unique within the house, in part because every room features these richly textured,

The decorative elements on the steel I-beam fireplace mantel look like rosettes hand fashioned by a blacksmith. Purchased as an off-the-shelf item at a bolt-supply store, these are malleable washers, also referred to as "bridge washers." As the name implies, the 3-in. washers are intended for use on bridges. In this house, they are used both structurally (outside to bolt the ledger beam and inside on the living room's ceiling to attach the angle iron to the wood beam) and decoratively (on the fireplace mantels). Here, they are spot-welded onto a steel surface, painted, then sealed.

The dining area features a set of built-in maple cabinets. While it's separate from the kitchen, the spaces are still connected, thanks to a pass-through between the cabinets.

The master bedroom, featuring a galvanized steel portico, enjoys its own entrance to the courtyard through French doors.

Out of the Box

The walls in the house look like plaster, thanks to a technique referred to informally as "poor man's plaster." Regular drywall is mudded and taped as usual, then the entire surface of the wall is skim-coated with gypsum mud mixed with a pigment. The walls are smoothed with a trowel before they are sealed. This technique creates a warm, uneven tone (in the living room, yellow and red pigments were mixed); and after sealing, the wall surface never needs painting.

inexpensive materials. For example, glass blocks are set singly in the hallway leading from the living area to the bedrooms. The blocks have an important function— to help control the strong western light—and they create a pattern on the long expanse of hallway.

And the master bedroom, which isn't luxurious, has been designed to be its own island in the house. Located at the end of the hallway, it has its own entrance to the courtyard through a set of French doors, which are marked on the outside by another set of drainage-pipe columns.

An honest use of materials

It's entirely possible to imagine this house with higher-end materials, like replacing the metal roof with shakes or tiles, the drainage-pipe columns with ornate concrete or carved wood, the steel angle iron in the living room with wood beams, or the concrete slab floors with hard wood. But such substitutions would ruin the home's character. It's the inexpensive materials, all presented and finished in a straightforward way, that give the home its style.

New School

From afar, it looks like a quaint New England house—clapboard siding with a cupola and a slate roof. But after taking a few steps closer, a visitor might begin to feel like Gulliver among the Brobdingnagians. The front path and the entrance door are massive, and this simple illusion transforms what is in fact a very large building into what looks like the quintessential old-fashioned home. When the couple purchased it in 1994, the old barn had been functioning as a school for more than 40 years. In its current incarnation as a spacious studio and living quarters for two artists, the structure has found a new form: a loft that looks like an overscale cottage.

There's every indication that this late-nineteenth-century building has a distinguished legacy. As part of an estate, its size indicates that it once had held numerous horses and carriages. When Peggy Diggs and Ed Epping purchased it, the building was occupied but in poor condition. The walls sloped alarmingly; a tree had punched a hole in the roof; there were creatures inhabiting the basement. Spending $48/sq. ft., the couple hired contractors to help with structural problems. But when it came to unearthing original floors and bead-board walls and ceilings, they did the work themselves. When the interior painting bid came in at $20,000, they took that on as well.

Using the philosophy of structure first, two artists restored an old barn, which had been converted to a school, into living and work space. To minimize the home's large scale, the architect suggested that it be painted one solid color.

reinterpret,
don't replace

1

Floor-to-ceiling shelves of books line a wall of the library. French doors lead down an artfully tiled hallway to the homeowners' dual art studios.

2

With 2,500 sq. ft. upstairs, there's a generous amount of shared space, which the couple has divided into areas for dining, reading, and entertaining.

On the floors in the high-traffic entrance area, the couple opted for vinyl tiles to combat the long muddy season in their Massachusetts area. Using four colors of basic 12-in. tiles and cutting them different sizes, Peggy Diggs played with patterns, creating a simple configuration for the floor. Then the tiles were professionally installed. The pattern, which is composed of rectangles and squares, transforms the floor and turns a practical solution into an artistic one.

The transformation is remarkable: the space feels natural and easy—there's little that's flashy or forced in the interior. Rather than try to impose their idea of how a house should be or function, the homeowners let the integrity of the structure inspire the renovation.

The architecture of archaeology

It was the process of renovation that unearthed the building's history. First to go were the layers of school—the apartments, the bathrooms, the classrooms, the gym. Later the remnants of the carriage house—the floors, the beams, and the hayloft—were revealed. For example, what had been the school's gymnasium (and before that a tack room, circa 1911) was covered with layers of cracking drywall on the ceiling and walls. Ed started stripping it down with the idea that it would be replaced before he discovered perfectly good bead board. The room now functions as a library.

Two existing classrooms on the lower level were transformed into the two studios. The problem was where to put the kitchen. Should it be located on the first floor, as it is in most houses, or should it be close to living and bedrooms, which would be more convenient but upstairs?

Architect Carlos Jimenéz helped the homeowners answer this and remake the existing space into a workable home. The original entrance was reconfigured to be more in scale with a house by adding an angled wall near the front entrance. The wall directs visitors up the stairs to where the kitchen now resides.

1

The curved wall that announces the entrance to the bedroom is a practical and aesthetic solution that architect Carlos Jimenéz designed to bring form and interest to what could have been just a long wall with a lot of doors.

2

Nooks tucked into the roof peaks provide smaller, cozier spaces within the larger expanse. The two guest bedrooms also fit easily under the slope of the roof.

Out of the Box

There were many items that were salvaged, these bathroom countertops among them. They were recycled from the chemistry lab at nearby Williams College. Made from Fireslate, they're almost half the weight of natural stone. This manmade material, which consists of Portland cement, silica sand, water, and fillers, makes a dark, rich countertop that fits in perfectly with the rough-hewn character of the Diggs and Epping home.

A room that opens up into one large space, the second level is a loft. Structural beams are the space's dominant architectural detail; they dot the room like a collection of interior trees and help frame functions within the large area: dining area, television nook, and living area. Palladian windows, from the structure's life as a school, distinguish the kitchen and television nook. The kitchen sits at one end of the loft; it's open to the rest of the room, but a half-wall hides dishes and preparation area.

The beams, which hearken the home back to its life as a barn, are still marked with "no smoking" signs, written many decades ago. Bedrooms are carved into small rooms off the main space that were originally meant for storage. Bathrooms, added when the building was a school, were kept but renovated to meet the needs of the new homeowners.

In its new life, this loft space doesn't feel like a school, or even like a barn. The renovation has brought forth the structure's integrity, transforming it into a light-filled place for work and home life.

Shipshape

Although it doesn't float, this house functions with the precision of a first-class sailboat and takes full advantage of the site's dramatic views of the Saratoga Passage.

It was built by an avid sailor and designed by an architect who not only spends his weekends sailing but also lives in a houseboat. There is, naturally, a shipshape quality to this contemporary home, inspired by an understanding of how to get the most out of small spaces.

The house was intended to be a weekend cabin on Camano Island, Washington, but it has now become a full-time residence for the homeowner, who built it in 2002 for $70,000. She did much of the finish construction herself, along with her partner; the two women worked with a consulting builder, who specializes in helping people build their own homes.

Architect Tim Carlander's design was actually the second version of the house. The first design, a shingle-style, builder-designed box, was in the process of being built when the homeowner decided she wanted something different. A serendipitous meeting with the architect at a sailing event brought in the team of Vandeventer/Carlander who were hired to design a home as special as the site. Because the foundation had already been dug, the architect had to work with the existing footprint, which was 16 ft. by 22 ft.

The approach to this cubist cottage—a geometric composition of galvanized metal, windows, and cement fiberboard—presents dramatic views of both sea and house.

26

Clad in dark gray cement fiber-board, this 352-sq.-ft. cabin is open to the views of mountains and sea through the 8-ft. by 8-ft. doors, but its privacy from neighbors is maintained by a corrugated galvanized steel wall.

A sloped shed roof makes room for a sleeping nook that is open to the living area below. With the low ceiling and ocean views, the room is like a berth on a boat.

Out of the Box

There's a detail on the exterior of the house that feels like pure whimsy—a panoramic slot cut into the galvanized metal wall. It frames a terrific view, and it's hard not to get a glimpse of what lies beyond. From inside the house, it functions as a peephole; a small corner window in the living area aligns precisely with the slot, allowing anyone in the kitchen to see coming vehicles.

1

Snug as a boat That footprint and the budget meant that the house would be small, so Tim looked at ways to make the space function efficiently but also appear spacious. The 352-sq.-ft. space feels much bigger because of high ceilings and clear connection to the outdoors.

And as in a boat, the sleeping quarters are snug. A ladder, purchased from a ship supply store, leads up to the loft, where the angle of the roof meets windows.

The kitchen is tucked under the loft, and just like a boat galley, everything is lined up along the wall. The owner opted for small-scale European appliances, which was an expensive splurge but the only option for the living area.

Clad entirely in sheets of maple plywood, the inside is warm and cozy. The owner could have chosen drywall for the walls, perhaps a cheaper alternative, but instead, she selected the prefinished maple ply, which is available off the shelf at local home-improvement stores. The coziness it lends is a good reminder that modern architecture is not always stark. It also allows for easy access

1

This one-room house takes advantage of the views of water. The interior is finished in light maple and darker cherry plywood.

2

The kitchen balances high-end European appliances with IKEA® cabinetry. The windows provide light and ventilation over the sink and stove areas.

When building a house, it can be disastrous (read: "costly") to change your mind. Not so for this homeowner, whose original plan was for a basic builder-designed cabin. Taking advantage of an offer of a free excavation—the local road was being cleared and the excavator was available—she found herself well on her way to building that cabin. The footings were dug and the stem wall was built. Then she decided she wanted a different kind of cabin. Rather than start over, the existing foundation wall was used as a frame to pour a concrete slab, complete with radiant heat.

to wiring; much like in a boat, the plywood panels can be unscrewed to allow access to any of the home's mechanical systems

Outdoor embrace

Considering how the boating model played a role in the interior design, perhaps it's inevitable that there should be such an easy connection to the outdoors. Two sets of large glass doors bring in views, and when the doors are open to the patios, the house expands to embrace the gorgeous setting. The 30-ft.-long galvanized wall turns a corner to create an exterior garden room, while shielding the house from wind and the property behind it.

The owner moved to this cabin from a 3,500-sq.-ft. house on a nearby island. She reports that the reduction in area has only improved the quality of her daily life. What the small size insists on is a life lived without the clutter of extraneous possessions; what it gives in return is what all good design can, be it house or boat—an efficient and beautiful pattern for everyday life and a connection to the sea and sky.

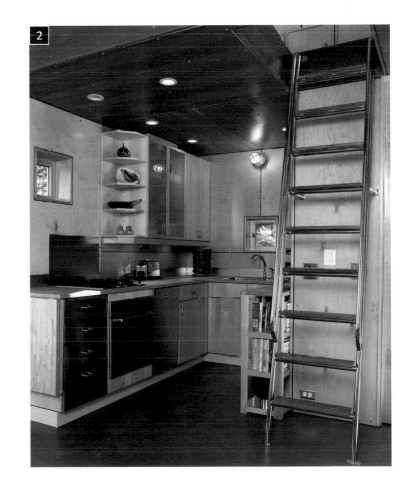

Mod

In Austin, Texas, a town that is no longer cool but hip, the price for a modest, urban bungalow is running about $300,000. What is a young (or old) hipster without a lot of cash to do? Enter KRDB (Krager/Robertson Design-Build), an architecture firm that sees potential in designing and building lower-end spec houses for a hungry populace in search of a good, cheap house.

The designers at KRDB are urban pioneers, and they have embraced east Austin, where real estate prices are still relatively low. Sold in 2004 for $180,000 (including land) to Ryan Jenkins and Mark Scheppe, this 1,650-sq.-ft. house with a black slate face sits on its modest block like a visitor from a very mod planet. By using the constraints of the site and a spare approach to design, KRDB created a house that combines the best of loft living within a single-family dwelling.

This flat-roofed house is perfectly in scale with its modest neighbors, but any resemblance ends there. Unconventional in form and composition, it brings the spare style of loft living to a single-family dwelling.

There's no question where guests enter, even though the entrance to the house is not on the front. A stucco wall, cypress lapping, and gravel path lead to the main door on the side.

The floor falls away as the house hugs the slope of the lot, which creates low intimate spaces and wide open living areas connected with a 75-ft.-long hallway that seconds as an art gallery.

Out of the Box

The house is designed like a loft, so the architects needed a simple way to divide the open space between public and private. The solution is a door made from wood slats and semitranslucent sandblasted acrylic that slides in and out of the guest bathroom. When it's pushed open, the door fits right on the bathroom's wall. Pushed out, it sections off the master suite from the rest of the house, while still allowing light to pass through.

Site-inspired shape

The lot the house is built on is narrow and deep with an almost 4 ft. of slope. Rather than regrade the site to make it level, the designers opted, for both aesthetics and cost, to design the house to fit the slope. With its long (nearly 90 ft.) and thin configuration, the house didn't work with a traditional front door. Instead, the architects created an entry to the property itself. A tall, white wall ushers visitors down a welcoming pathway. The path leads to a deck, and that is where you find the front door.

Cypress lap board, a design splurge used on the entrance side of the house, makes the approach lively with its rich honey color. It has the same long-lasting qualities as redwood. Much more inexpensive Hardiplank® board covers the other side and back.

Living in a loft

Laid out like a shotgun apartment, the home's private spaces (office, bedroom, and bath) are located toward the front, with the living, kitchen, and dining area at the back. The slope of the lot translates to different ceiling heights in the interior, and this simple effect transforms the house. It's the floor

2

1

The kitchen features stock items made special, like home-supply-store cabinet bodies replaced with birch plywood fronts and a slate-clad island.

2

The living area's smooth birch plywood interior paneling provides a counterpoint to the textured black slate inside and outside the house.

The slate that adds texture and contrast to the front of the house is actually a flooring material that the architects decided to put on the walls. The slate was applied much in the same way a shower is tiled, using a wood-framed wall with a waterproofing membrane and a cement fiberboard substrate. The slate was then sealed with a masonry sealer.

that falls away, though, not the ceiling that rises—the ceiling remains at the level dictated at the front of the house. And so as visitors walk through the house, it opens up to the soaring 13-ft.-high living space.

Front and back of the house are connected with a 75-ft.-long hallway, which is intended to show off art work. Clerestory and foot-level windows bring in light, and a simple and inexpensive ledge made of drywall adds detail to the long expanse of wall.

Inexpensive materials are used minimally to spice up the interior. The same black slate tile that wraps the front of the house continues on the inside wall of the master bedroom and into the kitchen. The living area features a wall clad in birch plywood. These two walls are like the yin and yang of the house—they're a contrast in warmth and texture, and they bring a great sense of destination to each end of the hallway.

In the kitchen, stock MDF (medium density fiberboard) cabinets have new fronts made from birch plywood, counters are Formica, and the island is covered with remnants of the slate. The windows are a mix of those that run floor to ceiling for backyard views and an assortment of smaller horizontal and vertical windows

marking the dining area. This room, with its high ceiling, simple detailing, and abstract window pattern is an entirely comfortable, inviting space—and a good reminder that design, that ineffable combination of proportion, light, and the quality of the space, can be created with a minimum of means.

Wee

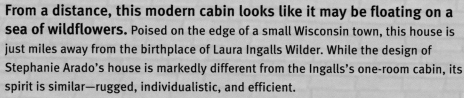

From a distance, this modern cabin looks like it may be floating on a sea of wildflowers. Poised on the edge of a small Wisconsin town, this house is just miles away from the birthplace of Laura Ingalls Wilder. While the design of Stephanie Arado's house is markedly different from the Ingalls's one-room cabin, its spirit is similar—rugged, individualistic, and efficient.

The owner, a classical violinist, wanted a meditative retreat that required little upkeep. The fact that the cabin is small, at 346 sq. ft., and has no electricity or running water appeals to her sense of adventure. But lifestyle issues aside, for the design of the cabin she requested something modern and bold. Architect Geoffrey Warner, intrigued with the idea of affordable modernist prefab structures, saw potential in the homeowner's $50,000 budget and determined to use the commission to design the prototype for a line of prefab houses.

In this weeHouse prototype, wood and glass conspire to create a space that is both cozy and modern. A rudimentary kitchen occupies one wall, while the sleeping quarters claim the opposite wall.

1

Taking advantage of the 16-ft. deck made from recycled plastic is one key to enjoying this modest-sized home in warm weather.

2

The interior is styled in part to look like an old-fashioned cabin with its tongue-and-groove fir on the floors, ceilings, and walls. The woodstove is the cabin's sole source of heat and adds a cozy centerpiece to the otherwise spare decor.

Built-in beds, including a bunk for a small child, are space-saving devices. But they also make a one-room cabin work by providing kid-scaled space for play. The niche below the bunk is also a great area for stowing away toys. There's a curtain that runs the length of both beds; it can be pulled for privacy or to hide a mess in a pinch.

Living in one room

Because prefab houses are built off-site then trucked in, the dimensions of a semi played a big role in the cabin's diminutive 14-ft. by 24-ft. size. But the layout is designed to make every bit of space work. Instead of breaking up functions, there's a shared interior space for the kitchen, living area, and bedrooms.

A built-in bed is tucked into one side, including a bunk for Stephanie's young son. A modest kitchen with stainless and enamel cabinets by IKEA sits across the room. It offers counter space, sliding glass shelves, and refrigerator for food storage. Exterior features—a deck and front porch—offer alternative places to hang out and make the interior feel larger, especially in warm weather.

The cabin features both newer, long-lasting, and inexpensive materials as well as classic cabin fare. The exterior looks as if it had been clad in metal, but it's actually Hardipanel, which has been finished with oxidized steel paint, a product often used for decorative architectural finishes. The sliding glass doors take the place of windows and help make the 8-ft. ceiling feel higher because they are tall, filling the cabin with sunlight. Inside, the floors and ceiling are finished in tongue-and-groove fir, which gives warmth without detracting from the home's clean style.

The line of prefab weeHouses that this prototype inspired is now on the market in various sizes, ranging from the 14-ft. by 24-ft. studio that Stephanie built to a 728-sq.-ft., two-bedroom unit. Not only is a weeHouse good and cheap, it's also fast to construct and can be inhabited in just 16 weeks. There are lots of variations available, including upgrades on interior finishes, complete kitchens, porches, and even stair units. Because the house is based on a simple cube configuration, it can be stacked or placed together in different ways.

1

1

From the living area, sliding doors invite views of the nearby wooded grove. The porch's slim steel cables for railings reflect the cabin's contemporary DNA.

2

Though it sits on the prairie, this modern cabin is on the frontier of design: it's prefab and it's cheap.

Out of the Box

In such a small space, large kitchen cabinets would simply take up too much room. The solution was to add peek-a-boo shelves with sliding glass fronts that can both block and display. These shelves are made from stained oak and sandblasted glass, but they look and function like shoji screens.

A place for meditation

For Stephanie, spending time here is not unlike spending time in any rustic one-room cabin: There's no television at the click of a remote or water at the turn of a faucet, and the charming outhouse in the back is the closest thing to an amenity. But unlike its counterparts (the fishing shack, the lean-to, the pioneer cabin), the weeHouse rusticity comes from its stripped-down form. The owner marvels at the peaceful quality of time spent here—the way the constant busyness of her city life is replaced by quietude, which allows her to pay attention to small miracles like a nest of baby swallows on the front balcony. This one-room retreat from modern life is, in fact, on the cutting-edge of design.

2

1

Metal Shop

Lee Gamelsky thinks of metal as a versatile, beautiful, and warm material. He is more than usually fond of it, admittedly because he grew up in a metallurgical shop in Queens, New York. Now an architect in Albuquerque, New Mexico, Lee is inspired by the material in almost every form—sheet, angle iron, or beam—and uses it in his work structurally and decoratively.

When it came to renovating his own home, an undistinguished concrete rambler from the 1950s, the architect and his wife, Sarah Frye, used the material to help them transform the old place into a contemporary home with a more amenable layout. With a budget of $60/sq. ft., the couple was determined to use the considerable skills they had—including finishing, staining, and pouring concrete—and to enlist a small crew to help with framing and construction. Employing a combination of unabashedly cheap materials, the renovation added 600 sq. ft. and essentially reoriented the house to take advantage of its location on the edge of a city park.

A 600-sq.-ft.-addition has brought a new face to a formerly undistinguished concrete-block rambler in Albuquerque, New Mexico. To bridge the two seamlessly, the addition was designed with materials from an industrial context: split-face concrete block, sheet metal, and glass block.

45

1

A freestanding closet space divides the living and dining areas. It also offers a niche for a home office, complete with a copper gutter, which the homeowner installed over his desk as a tribute to free-flowing ideas.

2

The architect designed simple, stylish sconces, which were fabricated from sheet copper by a metal shop. They hide basic porcelain keyless fixtures, adding style at a low price.

2

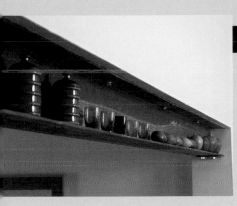

Out of the Box

The structural steel beam between living room and dining area has been left exposed, and it literally brackets the transition between the new and the existing spaces in the house. Perfect for displaying objects, the beam provides a sort of floating picture rail. It's just this sort of contrast—hard industrial edge of the beam and pretty composition of the artistic objects—that makes the renovation work so well.

Soft space, hard edges

The couple decided to keep what worked in the original house—the orientation of the bedrooms and kitchen—but to change the living room into a dining area and to add most of the square footage to the entrance and new living space. Lee designed a curved, arched, and entirely modern addition that contrasts well with the low-slung box shape of the old house.

The addition features the concrete block that composes the original house; but here it's split-face, which has a rough, stone-like texture. The one-story rambler now functions as a backdrop to the much more striking addition.

Perhaps what's most noticeable about the new entrance and living area is how three curves are at work: a ceiling that arches 14 ft.; a rounded half-wall by the door; and across the living room, a curving western wall, which is detailed with small glass blocks that filter out the strong sun and offer niches for display. The new room also has a built-in closet that provides space for a desk. With the addition of the closet, there is a sense of enclosure to the living area. Yet, even with such dynamic geometry, the main focus is the windows that look out to the park. The homeowners wanted to feel more a part of the community, and now, because their house faces the neighborhood, they do.

Copper details

The sheet copper seen on the front of the house also appears on the inside, echoing the industrial accents. In the kitchen, the backsplash is made from 24-gauge copper. The metal, which adds color and warmth to the room, was roughed up with steel wool to remove its protective layer then coated with an automotive sealer. Sheet copper was also used to fashion inexpensive sconces that hide basic porcelain keyless fixtures (the same type that holds a bare bulb).

adding on,
spending less

1
The sheet copper backsplash and concrete countertops, which were poured by the homeowners, add rich detail to an otherwise off-the-shelf kitchen.

2
The dining room, original to the house, flows into the new living and entrance addition, which now features windows on the front, providing views of the park beyond.

MATERIAL WORLD

The sheet metal that adorns the Gamelsky-Frye house is a relatively easy way to add a bit of instant style to a space. The copper on the outside is sealed to prevent it from oxidizing, which, in New Mexico's dry climate, would turn it to a dark brown color. A durable material that can last for up to 100 years, copper adds a rosy hue to the face of the house and contrasts nicely with the textured concrete block.

The rest of the interior received a minimal, inexpensive redo. For example, rather than replace the floors, the couple decided to strip them down to the original concrete subfloor. In an effort to incorporate the cracks into the finished surface, Lee ground the concrete, filled the cracks with grout, then stained and sealed the floor. The rich, mottled surface brings strong contrast to the wood and metal accents and highlights the home's contemporary style.

The surprising quality of the house is the warmth it exudes, given the fact that so many basic materials were used. With a playful touch, this formerly bland rambler has been transformed into an unpretentious and whimsical family home.

1

Starter Barn

Given the number of barn doors (two), what the architect calls yardarms, and the apparent loft (minus the hay), the logical conclusion is that Phil and Masey Kaplan live in a barn. Only this barn is not a drafty farm building that's been converted to luxury digs. It's Phil's own barn-like creation, one that cost him just $80/sq. ft. Phil, an architect, admits he would have built a spaceship if that would have given him the most room for his budget, but it was the barn's rectangular form that provided the greatest volume needed to accommodate a busy family life and space for home offices.

The house, which sits outside of Portland, Maine, is not your average barn. Some decidedly nontraditional details, like a soaring wall of windows, conspire to give the place a contemporary flair. Completed in 2002, the 3,200-sq.-ft. home is a playful and exuberant residence for a family of four and fits well into the neighborhood of traditional houses.

The barn form, with its shed roof and simple rectangular shape, meant construction costs would be relatively low. And to save further and minimize construction waste, the architect specified standard dimensions so that standard-size materials could be used.

At home in a barn: This new house combines the drama of a wall of windows with the comfortable style and materials of an American vernacular form.

The barn-door shutter is pulled over the windows from the outside. Its pattern of boards and cracks of light, with the X of the framing, make it look like a piece of modern art.

Like many affordably built homes, the interior space has few walls. More loft than barn, this living room features soaring ceilings and a wall of windows.

Out of the Box

The stone "foundation" wall at the front of the house is actually faux—real stone, but not structural. Not even attached to the house, the stones are tucked between the grade and the framing to simulate an old foundation. Under the window, the wall was made with dry-stacked stones that sit directly on top of the foundation and flush to the subsill of the glass.

1

And he figured he would build up, not out, to save money on the smaller foundation. Even though Portland municipal code says he was limited to a 35-ft. structure height, Kaplan was able to build a four-story home, which includes a walk-out basement.

The couple faced the challenge of creating an interior that wasn't just as big as a barn but that would balance the desire for intimate space with communal family space. (To connect the soaring ceiling to the living room, Phil designed a wall of windows, which face southern exposure.) The windows provide a striking focal point and add a tower of natural light that unifies all three levels. Home offices on the top floor are tucked into the peak of the roof, but overlook the space below. Even the master bedroom is connected with a cut-out interior window that brings in direct sunlight, ventilation, and a view of the activities below.

The first floor benefits from an open plan, with living area marked by windows and timbers. The kitchen and dining areas are tucked under the second-floor master bedroom and bath.

Two home offices—one for Phil, an architect, and the other for Masey, a graphic designer—are tucked up high on the third floor. The vintage ceiling beams are from a nineteenth-century barn.

The master bedroom, painted a vibrant color, has an interior window to allow for light and a view of the activities below.

Borrowed from a barn The house features
deliberate references to the farm building vernacular, some of which are functional and others that are purely decorative. Barn board, or no. 4 grade board-and-batten pine board, covers the exterior, it's also used inside on the stairwell and second level. Windows are mullioned and painted brick red.

No residential barn is complete without a barn door, and this house has two. A tall one on the front of the house features turnbuckles and can be pulled over the wall of southern windows to filter the light. The door is made from boards without battens, so the light streams through the gaps, evoking the romance of an old building. With such an expanse of southern light, the couple finds themselves closing the doors most often in the winter, when the sun is lower and the light can be quite intense. Another mini barn door inside can be pulled over the master bedroom cutout, for privacy.

The timbers that are used both structurally and decoratively throughout the house come from a nineteenth-century barn, by way of a client who was building a house out of the wood. The couple salvaged the leftover timbers and dropped everything to cart them away from the building site. The cost of $500 almost doubled by the time they paid for a truck large enough

ADVENTURES in Design

This three-season screen porch is made inexpensively from 12 stock screen doors. The dimensions of the porch were dictated by the size of a typical screen door, with a 2x4 column between each. A U-shaped channel on the columns, with two screws that can be easily removed, allow the homeowners to pop in glass doors when the weather gets cold. The doors sit on a low curb so that their tops reach high enough to bring in views.

A barn to the last detail: The house was roofed using a cost-effective alternative to standing-seam metal roofs. The galvanized metal is screwed down with self sealing screws over a water shield.

2

Made from a leftover timber, the coat rack greets visitors in the front hallway. The hooks are made from a collection of old hammers, which Masey bought on eBay® for $12.

2

to take the lumber to the building site, but the expense was well worth it.

The beams are used to add character to both the interior and the exterior. There's a timber on the south corner of the house that brackets the windows. A brace of floating timbers helps visually bring the 35-ft.-high volume to a more personal scale. And a timber brace and ceiling rafters enliven the home offices upstairs. The timbers, which are clearly old wood in a new space, are used as a design accent, referencing a barn without re-creating it.

A few expensive details For finishing

details, the Kaplans chose natural materials that would fit the interior's mixture of contemporary and traditional. The kitchen combines IKEA cabinets with slate counter-tops, because the couple wanted the hard stone finish to make their simple, off-the-shelf kitchen look more expensive.

Additional splurges include using wide planks of red pine for flooring and a solid oak front door, which befit an old country home. And while the quality of the front door is impressive, it's the coat rack, with its collection of old hammers, that's more eye catching. All the materials underscore the spirit of the American vernacular expressed in this extraordinary home; the coat rack communicates the home's sense of whimsy.

Bold

The house that Dan Rockhill designed for Roger Shimomura and Janet Davidson-Hues is big and bold. Its large size and concrete-and-metal form seem more informed by light commercial buildings than by residential architecture. Married in the mid-1990s, these two established artists needed a place where they could work and live together. After adding up the square footage requirements and examining the budget, Roger and Janet realized that they needed 5,000-sq.-ft. for about $250,000.

Both artists are also inveterate collectors of objects and fine art, but the space they wanted was generic—a word they used to describe a quality that would allow the art to speak louder than the architecture. They turned to Rockhill, who heads an architecture studio and teaching program at the University of Kansas and who is known for designing and building experimental structures. Long and fortress-like, the house he designed shields its occupants from the noise and distraction of a busy nearby parkway. In fact, the first view of the house, at least what's visible behind the trees, is of a massive concrete wall detailed with corrugated galvanized metal.

The butterfly roof makes a dramatic statement at the garage entrance of this unconventional house, with an oversize galvanized drain spout that collects water. The cladding is concrete tile veneered onto a stick-built frame.

59

This modern, muscular house provides work and living space for two artists. But in a reverse of typical needs, the workspace is 4,000 sq. ft. and living space is a much more streamlined 1,000 sq. ft.

High ceilings and white walls transform the living area into a gallery for art display, while the windows allow views of a small pond. The doll perched on the window is actually a department store mannequin.

MATERIAL WORLD

Finishing details count a lot in a house that is spare and modern. The doors and windows were important expressions of both entrance and light, and most conventional options weren't bold enough for the home-owners' taste. These doors, which balance welded steel and tempered glass, are usually used in factories. Here, they manage to look both heavy and delicate at the same time.

garages with a constructivist metal downspout, in which geometric planes create an abstracted and industrial-looking form. Entirely functional, it's a striking sculptural statement against the concrete backdrop.

Space simple
Much of the interior volume of the house is dedicated to studio space—in fact, 4,000 sq. ft. The remaining 1,000 sq. ft. is divided into living area, kitchen and dining room, one bedroom, and two offices. The living area features a two-story bank of steel-mullioned windows. They bring in views of a small pond and function in this house much as a fireplace would—as a place to gather, not around fire, but near light.

Concrete veneer
One exciting aspect on the exterior is a series of concrete panels that covers the house. The architect was looking for an inexpensive cladding that would be maintenance free, within the budget, and the proper scale for the wide expanse of space. To make sure the concrete panels were an exact fit and to save money, he poured each one on-site.

The 4-ft. by 6-ft., 1½-in.-thick tiles were fabricated from a mixture of cement and fiber additive, which acts as a binder. Tremendously heavy, each one took six men to carry, and was hung on 2-ft. by 6-ft. framing.

A galvanized metal cornice trims the house, with soffits welded out of steel to support the overhang. A butterfly roof reaches its dramatic conclusion above the

1

Art takes precedence over the architecture in the kitchen, which is functional and not luxurious, detailed primarily with the couple's collections.

2

In Janet's office, which is separate from her studio, the structure's sloped metal ceiling shapes the space. The partial wall allows light to enter from windows just beyond.

Out of the Box

Stainless-steel hand railings, found most often in hospitals and in bathrooms for the disabled, are transformed into a stair rail. The homeowners looked for one long stainless railing, but couldn't find it; they opted for three shorter handrails. It's a fitting choice: The stainless says "industrial," is very inexpensive, and matches the galvanized metal that finishes the stairwell.

Along with the kitchen, the living area benefits from a slope in the lot. The ceilings are high, which provides lots of white walls for display. The couple's collections (including memorabilia from China's Cultural Revolution, 1950s chalkware carnival prizes, and salt and pepper shakers) are displayed throughout, but primarily in rooms where there isn't much light, so the objects are protected from damaging ultraviolet rays.

Although the interior is indeed simple, it's actually far too interesting and welcoming to be considered truly generic. One splurge was wooden floors in the living area, which add color and offset the coolness of the concrete exterior. The ceilings also add interest; they are covered in corrugated galvanized metal, which saved the expense of installing drywall at such a height.

Designed as a backdrop for its occupants and their art, the house is a unique and entirely brave new home: one that redefines the balance between work and life and also manages to be an expression of the people who create within it.

Music

It's called a "farm road," where the tall red house is located, even though there aren't many farms left. Like much of the land within commuting distance of the Twin Cities, the area is caught in the transition between rural prairie and suburban sprawl. This house, designed for a musical couple, is full of surprises. There's something familiar about it, even though it's not a barn or a farmhouse or anything remotely suburban. The tall building, painted barn red, with exaggerated peaked rooflines and overscale dormers, is a modern riff on rural structures.

The house and studio, built by David and Lori Folland, who both grew up in farming communities, was designed to integrate elements of their pasts with expressions of who they are now. As a luthier, David transforms wood into one-of-a-kind stringed instruments played by professional musicians around the world. Lori, a classical pianist, spends much of her day playing music. They both wanted their home to express the same approach to art and craft they insist on in their work. The problem was that their mortgage of $230,000 (in 2000) could not begin to pay for either the materials they wanted, or the skilled craftsmen required.

The approach to this modern–vernacular house, which was designed for a musical couple, reveals its careful composition of peaked roofs and dormers.

A **stair screen** made from maple plywood adds rich detail to the front entrance. Lori uses the house as her studio; her grand piano sits just off the living room.

Hunting and gathering Locus

Architecture, a design and build firm based in Minneapolis, conceptualized a tall, narrow form for the house, a money-saving strategy. The smaller footprint would mean a smaller foundation, which is generally more expensive by the foot to build than the framing. And then the couple began to investigate ways to buy expensive materials for a cut-rate price.

Salvage shops yielded the wood for the framing of the house. More recycled wood came from a farmhouse demolition just down the road. The Follands removed the pine sheathing, which they reused in the studio's ceiling, as well as enough fir to finish the second and

Filled with artful design and hand-crafted details, the house features 30 recycled windows and almost 5,000 lin. ft. of wood reclaimed from an old farmhouse.

The kitchen bridges living and dining rooms; it's distinguished by a plywood ceiling with inset lights and the cherry cabinets made by David and his father.

1

The top floor of the home is a retreat from work, where the couple can read and relax. The built-ins, made from recycled wood, fit nicely in a space made unusual by the various roof angles.

2

The bedrooms are upstairs, where a nook made by the large dormer offers enough room for yoga practice. The boards under the railing were salvaged from the farm where David grew up.

Out of the Box

No ordinary set of stairs, this plywood ship's ladder is both funky and functional. It leads up to the house's top floor. The risers alternate and are indeed straight; but they are angled along the front edge, which, with the handrail, creates a sense of forced perspective.

third floors of the house. For the windows, they went to a trash bin in nearby Northfield, where they found 30 perfectly good windows from a remodel of an Odd Fellow's building.

There was still the expense of hiring skilled labor, which in many instances is the most costly part of working with materials like wood and stone. Inspired by the way rural buildings used to be built, the couple assembled a group of people willing to participate in what can only be called a modern-day barn raising.

As a stringed-instrument maker, David, Is a skilled woodworker and did much of the finish carpentry. He was able to enlist the apprentices in his shop, family members, and people in the community who wanted to learn woodworking skills in return for working on his house. It took almost a year to build, but the end result is the structural equivalent of a fine instrument.

Filled with unique details

The house is just over 2,000 sq. ft., not big by any means, but its different levels make it feel quite spacious. Each floor has unique detail. An organic, nature-inspired stair screen crafted from maple plywood greets visitors at the front door. Upstairs, the tall, thin dormer on the front of the

The studio for making instruments is essentially one big room with a small loft for wood storage. The high ceilings make for an inspirational workspace with terrific acoustics, a place meant for music.

ADVENTURES in Design

The limestone David Folland planned to use for his foundation was relatively cheap, but the labor involved in stacking was not. So rather than hire stonemasons, he contacted an industrial arts teacher from the local high school and enlisted a group of students from the school who were eager for some hands-on experience. Along with their teacher, they learned the mortarless technique of drystacking from the architects. Working during what would be class time and with Folland running the project, the crew completed the walls over a six-month period.

house brings in a two-story column of light. On the second level, there's a nook where Lori does yoga. A ship's ladder, fashioned from maple plywood, leads to yet another floor. Tucked into the peak of the roof, this room features a built-in table with benches and a window seat for one.

Next door, a studio
The studio echoes the house's peaked form, but not the different levels. Its 700 sq. ft. is enough space for materials, tools, and an apprentice or two, all under a soaring, vaulted ceiling. The height makes it feel like a church, and also offers fantastic acoustics.

If you're lucky, a visit to the Follands' house and studio will bring you there when you might hear someone test driving a new violin or Lori playing Bach on the piano. That's if the windows are open. If you miss out on the background score, the house will still sing, in a purely visual way. Built by two people who were willing to use every ounce of ingenuity and persistence they had, this is a house that many people in the community can also point to with pride. Filled with beautiful materials and an old-fashioned approach to craft, it's a good reminder of what the confluence of creativity and constraint can build.

Three

The approach to this compound in Tuscon, Arizona, might baffle first-time visitors. For starters, there are three mailboxes—all sharing the same address. Instead of a big facade to announce an entrance to the street, there's a retro-style concrete-block and aluminum gatehouse. Push open a blue metal gate and, as the geometric forms of this compound unfold, bursts of color, energetic angles, and a flourishing desert courtyard reveal themselves. The answer to those puzzling mailboxes and the almost nondescript concrete-block front is found in an unconventional living arrangement: The house that Frank Mascia built is, in fact, three homes—one for his wife, Jeanne Taylor; one for himself; and one for his aging parents, which now serves as rental property.

Built from block, stucco, and galvanized metal, this enclave is proof that the quality of a space has little to do with luxury appointments and everything to do with basic design decisions, such as the proportions of the rooms, the number and placement of windows, and how the structure is integrated into the landscape. Built for $80/sq. ft. (including a swimming pool) in 1998, these three structures meet the needs of a blended family by allocating living spaces for distinct purposes.

A city lot in an older Tuscon, Arizona, neighborhood features three homes, one for each member of a couple and a rental apartment. Private at the front, the property unfolds with exuberant colors and shapes.

Frank wanted the feeling that a broad expanse of glass brings to the interior and came upon an ingenious solution that allows for large windows throughout Jeanne's house. Rather than specify custom tempered-glass windows, he mounted sliding-glass doors in standard sizes with door hardware at window height. Framed like aluminum windows, they glide open easily.

1

No frills, please

Jeanne's house is striking in its Zen-like simplicity. At 1,400 sq. ft., it's big enough for her and for the combined dining and entertaining functions of the couple. Pigmented stucco, concrete block, and glass are used on the outside; the same inexpensive materials are used inside as well. Concrete covers the floors; the expansive glass windows in the living room and kitchen are sliding-glass patio doors hung at window height.

Because the interior is so simple and spare, color and curves resonate. Used at the entrance, these elements create an immediate impact. The two saffron-colored curved walls near the front door bracket the kitchen area. They shield food preparation from the dining space, yet allow the cook to socialize with her guests. A bright purple rectangle on the living room wall encases the guest bedroom's pocket door and brings balance to the home's decorative composition.

Throughout, Jeanne's home epitomizes a well-conceived, economic floor plan. A built-in desk tucked into one end of the kitchen makes for a home office with views of the desert patio. The kitchen countertop, too, was carefully considered to create another space for informal meals; it extends over the cabinets to provide room for stools. Although the bedrooms are modest in size, the closets are quite generously proportioned, proving the adage that you can live small only if the closets are big.

A pad across the way

For his own home, Frank resorted to the notion of a pad, opting for utilitarian over flash. At 900 sq. ft., Frank's low-slung house is

1

There's nothing high-end about this kitchen, but it works well and allows the cook to feel connected to guests. Gray Formica echoes the mottling of the concrete floors.

2

This floor plan epitomizes well-considered space. A home office is built into the far end of the kitchen area; the glass doors mounted as windows connect it to another patio off of the space.

2

1
The front porch off of Jeanne's house is angled for views of the courtyard and her husband's home across the way. With interior spaces kept small, the porches and patios virtually double the square footage of the house.

2
The living area of Frank's house is where the couple meets to watch television. There's no dining room here, just a counter extension where he can grab a quick bite.

Out of the Box

According to Frank, the fence that surrounds the back pool cost about an eighth of the price of a block and stucco wall. Inexpensive corrugated galvanized roofing panels were installed onto a painted steel tube frame with self-tapping screws. The metal fence, which is also used on the garage in the back, divides the house from the back alley.

made of concrete block and galvanized corrugated metal. It plays second fiddle to his wife's dynamic, angled structure across the courtyard.

The inside provides just enough common space, a niche of an office, and a utilitarian kitchen. Space is saved in the hallways by combining door functions—louvered sliding doors either cover the closets, or the adjacent bedroom and bathroom door frames.

Frank's living room is cozier than Jeanne's. Bookshelves do double-duty and extend far enough to become a counter for eating. The office is the size of a closet; but it functions efficiently, thanks to a built-in Formica-topped desk. The bedroom is simple but for the interesting low windows, which allow Frank to observe the courtyard from his bed.

The patio plan
The houses are small, and so is the lot—at just over half an acre; what is so astonishing is how private each person's home feels and yet how connected it is to the other buildings. The privacy comes from the geometry of Jeanne's house, which not only brings great energy to the architecture of the compound but creates small pockets on the edges of the lot, which are filled with patio gardens. There are three bordering Jeanne's house alone. In fact, there's a great balancing act at work in these structures between private and public, and it's beautifully arranged so that one can feel alone

or connected to the other houses without pulling blinds or hiding in the back.

When it comes time to relate with the other members of the family, the most popular meeting place has proven to be the swimming pool, where the couple takes a dip together every evening. It functions here as an oasis in the desert—a place to cool off at the end of the day and reconnect with one's spouse.

Florida

Anthony Vallée describes the home he designed and lives in with his wife, Susan, as a "Florida house." The home is indeed located in Florida's panhandle, where the landscape is both beach and piney woods—but Anthony is referring to something more than location. A Florida house, at least the way this one presents itself, is designed to balance interior space with outside rooms for living.

Built for $135,000 (including a swimming pool) in 2001, the house features materials like wood, concrete block, and as much glass as possible—all put to use on a flat-roofed, streamlined modern form. Materials such as concrete block and pine are found both on the interior and the exterior, reinforcing the sense that the spaces are interchangeable.

At the home's entrance, a stained pine exterior wall draws visitors inside. The wood echoes the pine trees on the lot, and it brings rustic warmth that extends inside in both the kitchen and the bath, creating a focal point in each room.

Florida's warm climate is the perfect excuse for a flat roof, which helps give the house its modern mien. The roof is made from structural steel, and it extends 10 ft. over the patio, creating a covered outdoor room.

1

The clerestory melts into its surrounds with the help of sky blue frames that blur the distinction between architecture and outside.

2

A view from the patio shows the modest kitchen niche, which is marked with a curved partial wall. Concrete floors unify the space, whether it's being used for cooking, dining, living, or sleeping.

ADVENTURES in Design

Anthony grew up in Miami, Florida, and nostalgic for the old neighborhoods there, he designed a variation on the classic driveway that features a strip of grass down the center. Two sets of tire curbs lead to parking spots for each car. Anthony poured the concrete curbs around pavers that were laid in the proper formation.

Concrete block is used on the other main interior wall, and it continues outside, where it defines one edge of the courtyard. The block, which is sandblasted for a surface that is rougher than the standard factory finish, completes the visual connection between the two spaces. Both materials are coarse, given the modern form—but Anthony knew that sleek modernism, with its terrazzo floors and refined materials, was out of his price range. What he opted for, instead, was to embrace rougher, less expensive materials and use them in a straightforward way throughout the house.

The floors are poured concrete, and they bear the distinctive pattern of two separate pours. While many people strive for a uniform appearance in a concrete floor, the Vallées were pleased with the swirling mottled affect, which occurred when separate batches of concrete were mixed. Anthony notes that the happy accident makes the floor's surface look more like marble and is nicely in keeping with the home's eclectic style.

1

1

The ceilings on the patio are composed of plywood, painted a light blue. The patio faces the swimming pool and a courtyard.

2

Lots of glass in the form of three sliding doors, a matching ceiling and roof, and a running concrete wall connects the indoors with the open-air courtyard.

1

Out of the Box

In their search to take every advantage of Florida's warm climate, the Vallées put the shower outside. While the cast-in-place concrete tub is inside, the shower head is found through the 9-ft. by 9-ft. sliding-glass door. The stained pine wall, which distinguishes the bathroom vanity, extends outside as well. The shower's "floor" is a combination of concrete and the herb pennyroyal, which releases a sweet, minty scent.

An inside outside house

The inside is a modest 745 sq. ft., a concession to the budget. The couple shares a multipurpose room, which functions as living room, kitchen, and—with a Murphy bed—master bedroom. There's a spacious bathroom down a short hall. Concrete floors, glass, a curved wall with niches in it for kitchen appliances, and an inherited sideboard complete the spare interior. The glass reinforces the sense of extended space.

There are actually three distinct outdoor areas. The flat roof extends over a large patio, which is covered with concrete pavers and gravel. The courtyard consists of the same concrete with grass planted between, in a pattern that mimics tile or carpeting. And then there's the swimming pool, without which no Florida house is complete.

A pavilion in a courtyard

From anywhere on the patio, the courtyard, or the pool, the interior is visible, thanks to sliding glass doors. With the doors open, the house becomes a pavilion set within a courtyard. The seamless blending of inside with outside is especially clear in the bathroom, which features a poured-in-place concrete tub and a sliding glass door that leads to the outdoor shower.

The idea of a courtyard was important to the couple, although they both concede it's not yet complete. They plan to build a bigger home when finances and family size increase. It will be sited on the other side of the swimming pool. The house they live in now will become guest quarters. At present, life in this small unique house, with its distinctive embrace of outdoor space, has shown them the best of both Florida and modern.

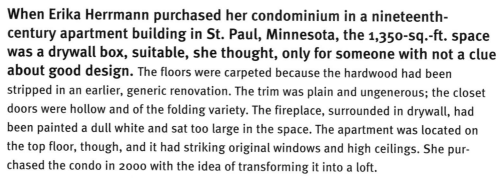

Loft

When Erika Herrmann purchased her condominium in a nineteenth-century apartment building in St. Paul, Minnesota, the 1,350-sq.-ft. space was a drywall box, suitable, she thought, only for someone with not a clue about good design. The floors were carpeted because the hardwood had been stripped in an earlier, generic renovation. The trim was plain and ungenerous; the closet doors were hollow and of the folding variety. The fireplace, surrounded in drywall, had been painted a dull white and sat too large in the space. The apartment was located on the top floor, though, and it had striking original windows and high ceilings. She purchased the condo in 2000 with the idea of transforming it into a loft.

The first thing she did was rip up the carpet and install maple floors in the living room and hallway. Then she called in an architect who had done an irreverent and inexpensive renovation of one of her favorite coffee shops. Geoffrey Warner's job was to add style and character for $30,000.

A bland condo was reborn as a loft. The renovation made the most of the bones of the space—high ceilings, good windows—and then imbued it with an eclectic, contemporary flair.

1

Rustic in appearance, this custom-made dining room light echoes the overall style of the apartment. Fabricated from two pieces of old wood, rope, and a line of halogen bulbs, it epitomizes the creative application of everyday materials.

2

By removing the wall to the kitchen and opening up an old acrylic bubble skylight, to reveal the rafters, the architect was able to bring more light into the condo.

ADVENTURES in Design

It happens in nearly every renovation: An ugly structural truth is uncovered. In this case, it was the cooking vent from the apartment below. Rather than reroute it, the architect and homeowner decided to embrace the problem and make the stack look integral to the kitchen. The resulting post does just that. Covered in a patchwork of shiny galvanized and matte-finish Galvalume® scrap, it's a receptacle for magnets and holds the phone.

Repeating the mantra "No, you can't afford that," the architect approached the renovation as a creative reinterpretation of the existing space, using inexpensive materials like plywood, diamond plate steel, and sandblasted acrylic.

Delete and replace The too-narrow baseboard trim was replaced with 5-in. slices of ApplePly®. The new trim was attached with exposed nickel-plated steel screws and finish washers—a detail that brought a lot of personality and saved the time of filling all the nail holes. The front door, steel and bland, was kept but was framed with wide bands of the same plywood trim. Now the door is a prominent entrance instead of one that faded away against the white walls.

2

open spaces,
careful choices

1

The library is simply a space off the living room, carved out by an artistic arrangement of black steel sheets and IKEA bookcases. The window seat is simplicity itself: folded steel and plywood.

2

The fireplace serves as a sculptural room divider. Original to the space, it's been revived with diamond plate steel, sandblasted acrylic, and a touch of aluminum plate.

The plywood used throughout this renovation is called AplePly, which is made with an alder core and a maple veneer face. The contrasting colors of the wood bring visual interest to the borders, which is why it is favored for finishing. The reason for the name? To make it sound American, as in "apple pie," and to distinguish it from imported plywoods.

The kitchen's transformation involved the only structural change, which was to open the room up to the dining and living spaces by removing a wall. The kitchen is spare and funky at the same time, with IKEA elements mixing with diamond plate steel and plywood. The countertops are Fireslate, a material that costs a third of the price of high-end counter materials (and is familiar to anyone who took a high-school chemistry class). Made from a pressurized mixture of portland cement, silica sand, and water, Fireslate is a product that can be used much like granite and Corian®; it comes in different widths and a variety of profiles.

The existing fireplace has been streamlined and reinterpreted as a diamond steel–clad piece of sculpture. Plywood box niches were placed around it for the homeowner's keys, mail, and CDs. A faux hearth, opposite of the real one and clad in aluminum diamond plate, makes a convenient spot for storing firewood. The chimney flue is surrounded in semitranslucent acrylic that reveals a wooden framework and glows in the evening when the fire is lit. Even the skylight has been reworked: It now shows off exposed metal ductwork and beautiful old ceiling rafters.

Affordable finishing touches

Originally, a nook off the living room seemed to be wasted space. With the simple addition of IKEA bookcases and sheets of black steel, the area has become a library. A bench made from folded steel and plywood created a built-in window seat.

The chandelier in the dining room is also architect-designed, and it epitomizes the sleight of hand at work in this renovation. It looks expensive but it's made from two old ceiling rafters, some rope, and halogen bulbs.

By using low-cost materials consistently and creatively and rethinking existing functions, a drywall box has been transformed into a decidedly new-world home.

River House

In this part of middle Tennessee, where land is sold by auction, this particular acreage, near the flood-prone Tennessee River flats, was dirt cheap. Architect Carson Looney saw that with the proper design, a house could be sited to embrace views of the river and avoid the rising water. Working with an inexpensive palette of materials, he knew he could use some design basics to create a house that would be an easy, informal getaway for his family.

The rectangular floor plan for the 1,500-sq.-ft. house is defined by standard-size materials, which helped keep costs to a minimum. For one, there was little or no waste and, two, Carson didn't have to pay to have lumber cut to fit. Most of the materials used reflect this cost-consciousness. The roof is metal, the cladding is Hardiplank, the windows are vinyl, and the shutters made from durable PVC (polyvinyl chloride) plastic.

Carson knew that the most striking feature of the property would be the river itself. The home was designed to take every advantage of the location and was built with some sweat equity in 2002 for $80/sq. ft. As a point of comparison, a similar house he designed that was completed in 2004, using available plans and without homeowner participation, was built for $109/sq. ft.

This **four-level house** was designed with elevated living spaces to capture views of the Tennessee River and to provide protection from floodwaters. A porch that wraps around the second level provides a few steps up to the front door.

1

The **stairway** to the master bedroom is clad in the same yellow pine as the living area. The steep, painted stairway leads up to a crow's nest.

2

Good views, no floods
The house sits on concrete-filled Sonotubes®, which elevate the home about 9 ft. and create a garage of sorts, where the family stores recreational vehicles. The massive pillars protect against water damage, and the height means that the home's living spaces are in prime river-viewing position. Treated timbers surround the perimeter of the house, supporting the porch, and provide a more delicate and decorative set of columns.

From inside, the views of the river are panoramic, in part because the house is sited in such a way that neighboring houses cannot be seen. As a result of the architect's careful consideration, the porch that wraps around the second level was lowered so that the railings would not obstruct the scene.

Material ease
There's something very comfortable about this weekend house. Both interior and exterior materials were chosen for low maintenance and ease of installation. The walls are covered in southern yellow pine boards, which needed no painting; the light golden color of the wood brings warmth. This 1-in. pine is not an expensive wood, and the boards were easier to install than hanging drywall. The floors are dog- and kid-proof, thanks to ceramic tile, which cost $2/sq. ft.

3

2

The fireplace is set at an angle to create a focal point, and the television hides away in a pine cabinet that also stores firewood.

3

From the living room, visitors can enjoy a bird's-eye view of the Tennessee River just outside through oversized windows.

1

Architect Carson Looney wanted the focus in the living area to be on the views instead of on the kitchen activities.

2

Looney also functioned as a developer for this parcel of land. His design for this house proved to be popular, and it's been copied with a few variations.

3

In a home that features an open and casual floor plan, this room, with its panoramic views of the treetops, is a private retreat.

ADVENTURES in Design

Because the kitchen was open to the rest of the house, the architect wanted to tuck it visually away. There are only a few cabinets, but there was still the need to store appliances and essentials. This nook slipped under the stair does just that: It's detailed like the rest of the kitchen but hides dishes and a microwave. A set of drawers are cleverly set into the stairwell and used for tableware storage.

1

The one splurge in the house proved to be the kitchen. Open to the rest of the living area, much of the kitchen is tucked against the far side of the room. Both the refrigerator and the stovetop are European because the homeowners were looking for quality on a small scale. Granite covers the counters, which, although relatively expensive, adds a flash of luxury to the diminutive kitchen. The cost was partially offset by the use of laminate cabinets. To further camouflage the space, the fancy refrigerator sits in a cabinet to make it look more like furniture. The kitchen work area extends into a niche in the stairway, which hides small, necessary appliances from view.

Private escape In such an open house, there needed to be at least one space to escape to—a private place for adults or kids to enjoy. That escape has turned out to be a small loft that sits on the very top floor. It's a bit like a crow's nest, with three sides of windows, and it provides the best river views in the house. The space epitomizes the sense of comfort that only good design can bring. Predicting the way the house would be used, Looney planned for a quiet getaway within this river retreat.

Log House

The moral of this story is look carefully before you demolish.

The building in question sat on a rundown piece of property outside of Bozeman, Montana, that had a creek running through the backyard. But the house—well, it was so beyond repair that even a real estate agent could not use the word *potential*. Everyone assumed that architect Ben Lloyd would tear it down and build again. And then a discovery was made: Underneath the ugly asphalt-shingle siding was a log cabin. It wasn't the typical Lincoln Log® variety, but a 1930s version of stacked logs with chinking in the seams; and while most everything else seemed to need replacing, Ben opted to save and keep the beautiful old logs.

The renovation was substantial, involving not only the foundation but also the home's mechanical systems. It was accomplished by Ben, his father, his brother, and a few plumbing and electrical contractors. Rebuilt for $50,000, this house features recycled materials that mingle with modern touches—all co-existing happily in the original log cabin shell.

A 1930s-era log cabin outside of Bozeman, Montana, has been transformed into a new house through sweat equity. The metal cladding was reclaimed from a shed on the property; the windows and door frames are made from Galvalume.

ADVENTURES in Design

By essentially making an aluminum frame out of sheet metal, the architect solved a problem that is often encountered when replacing windows in an old structure: The window may be plumb, but the opening can look crooked. Galvalume was scored and folded—almost like making a box—and then lined with plywood for strength on the sides. The log face of the house was trimmed to receive the metal. Later, the metal was fitted into the cuts, and the logs were re-chinked up to the edge. The detail, which unifies all the windows, adds a modern touch to a formerly rustic exterior.

Save and reuse The homeowner determined that while he would essentially be building a new house, he would reuse as many materials as he could, not just to save money but because he recognized that a few weather-worn details added patina and beauty. For example, the stones from the original fieldstone foundation, which was replaced with proper footings, are now a path that leads to the house. The interior doors were rescued from a school that was being torn down and were a bargain at three for $15. They're hung on barn-door hardware and function like pocket doors to save space.

Inside, a sea green sliding door was made from a panel salvaged from an old lean-to on the house. Even a sheet of rusted corrugated metal, destined for the trash pile, was used over the backdoor, creating a dramatic accent against the dark logs. Old ceiling joists intersect with a new steel beam, which was used to hoist the cabin off its original foundation. The ceiling is now open in the center of the space, which creates a visual pause between kitchen and living room.

1

There's little evidence of log cabin inside the home. Strategies toward making small spaces modern are at work throughout, from the varied ceiling heights to the bold use of color.

2

Inside, new materials mingle with salvaged ones. The green door, with its rich patina, was made from a piece of an old lean-to. The sliding maple door was reclaimed from a high school that was being torn down.

2

1

The stove is original to the log cabin, but the eye-catching vent is new. The quilted pattern adds an old-fashioned feel to this retro kitchen.

2

Like the rest of the house, the kitchen is a study in the resurrected and the new. The refinished pine floor, formerly the subfloor, Coronado stove, and exposed rafters blend well with off-the-shelf cabinetry.

Out of the Box

The shower stall in Ben's cabin is made from galvanized metal, and the materials cost just $75. It's warm in the winter and cool in the summer, because the metal conducts the water temperature almost instantly. The process involved using a standard tile shower base. A metal shop then cut the galvanized sheet to the specifications of a template. The pieces were attached with metal roofing screws and silicone.

1

Old outside, new inside

Inside there's little evidence of the original structure. Ben wanted it to feel like a contemporary house, not a log cabin, so he covered the walls with drywall. To help it function like a modern space with an old-fashioned sense of style, he opened up the living area to the kitchen, making it all feel larger.

The kitchen is small, but convenient. Ben used IKEA cabinets and storage items but kept the cabin's old gas stove, which had a retro style that appealed to him.

The stove vent faces the living area. Rather than go for something that was purely practical, Ben opted for a piece of sheet metal that was quilted by his local metal shop. The lively pattern is reminiscent of an old diner. In a house that mixes the past and present so beautifully, it's right at home.

Box

The first Flatpak house, a modern box of glass, concrete, and wood, now sits in a gracious neighborhood in Minneapolis, Minnesota. It's hard to believe that this house was put together like a kit, and that all its parts arrived on palettes, were craned into place, and then finished by a small crew. The innovative house is the brainchild of architect and homeowner Charlie Lazor, who sees it as the future of good, cheap house design.

Charlie is not a beginner when it comes to creating good, affordable design. Along with John Christakos and Maurice Blanks, he founded a line of inexpensive furniture called Blu Dot to answer what they saw as a market need. The success of the Blu Dot line proved that, in the world of commodities, design can be affordable.

This house is the prototype for the Flatpak house system, which will sell for about $140/sq. ft., a price that includes the cost of foundation, cabinets, appliances, general contracting services, and in-floor heating system. And just as consumers are able to pick the material and color in the Blu Dot furniture line before it's constructed, they are given a menu of choices with the Flatpak house. The consumer is presented with a variety of options in square footage, footprint, and materials, which can change the face as well as the feeling of the home's design.

The prototype Flatpak house, a kind of architectural kit, presents a cool composition of Douglas fir, cement board, glass, concrete, and black steel doors. It looks like an architect-designed contemporary home—not outlandish, but very much a house for the twenty-first century.

1

The office is set apart from the house and benefits from light on both sides; upstairs, there's a guest bedroom. When buying this home, consumers can opt to switch out this separate structure for a garage.

2

The kitchen is streamlined and efficient, with sleek appliances and sealed zinc countertops. The concrete floors are installed as panels, and radiant heat keeps them cozy.

2

ADVENTURES in Design

The Flatpak configuration features a combination of panels that are sheer and solid. How they're put together depends on what degree of privacy the homeowner is looking for. In this house, there's lots of glass on the side that faces the neighborhood to make the house feel friendly and open. There's also glass at the end, near the living room. But the back of the house looks onto a busy bike path, so the Lazors opted for more solid panels there.

Mix and match

The Flatpak house differs from prefab houses, because it's not built off-site and then delivered. Rather, its components are manufactured off-site, and then it's built with panels that are bolted together, insulated, and wired. Later, they are completed with an interior fiberboard wall surface that's been finished with epoxy paint. Even the foundation is radically different from typical construction methods.

The concrete arrives in panels that have been insulated. The stud walls are then attached to holes drilled into the surface of the panels, which saves time. It takes about 24 hours for cranes to put the panels in place, as opposed to the days needed to pour and cure a basic concrete foundation. These panels make up the entire house: from foundation to windows, from exterior walls to roof. In fact, the roof panels include a metal surface, insulation that exceeds the R-value for even the most extreme northern climate, and a white metal interior cladding for the ceiling.

The first Flatpak feels as if it had been custom-designed for the Lazor family's up-to-the-minute needs. The children, who are young, can roam freely in the open downstairs, from the dining area to the kitchen to the living room space. The upstairs has a large playroom to offset the small, efficient bedrooms.

Out of the Box

The wall surfaces at work in this child's bedroom are stained medium-density fiberboard (MDF) and sand-blasted glass, which isn't visible. Eventually, when the child wants more privacy, the glass can be changed to an opaque surface. All of the bedrooms feature built-in cabinets and drawers made from stained and sealed MDF; so even though they are small, there's no need for closets and dressers.

Some of the walls upstairs are semitransparent sandblasted glass, which creates a connection between kids and parents. The walls can be easily replaced with another material like birch plywood, a little like the way one snaps together a Lego® piece. There's a home office, which is in its own little structure, and a guest room, which sits on top and is accessed through a covered walkway attached at the home's second level.

With a few changes, this house, which is one of four prototype configurations, would work just as easily for a retired couple with lots of visiting grandchildren. But what won't change is the feeling of the house, which is generous, light filled, and clean: It's not the sort of house that dictates the style of the furniture, nor does it constrain life with any kind of rigidity. The Flatpak house is what Charlie calls "manufactured architecture"; unlike most houses on the market today, it puts architecture right on the shelf.

1

The architect refers to the home office as the "sanctuary." It's separated from the main house but is accessible through a covered deck. A glass bridge connects the space to the home's second floor.

2

Upstairs, the material and configuration of the walls can be changed. The light fixture is made from halogen bulbs and two engineered wood beams.

Alt.house

For a couple who founded an arts and humanities Web site, it should be no surprise that they dubbed their new home "alt.house." Sited in a suburban enclave outside of Bozeman, Montana, the house is simple, respectful of its split-level and ranch-style neighbors, but entirely different in its details and approach to interior spaces. A practical, affordable alternative, the house presents a powerful reinterpretation of the typical suburban dwelling.

Designed by architect Patrick Larum, the house was built in 2000 for $149,000 with work on a few finishing details completed by the homeowners. With its gable roof and rambler shape, this 2,500-sq.-ft. home not only speaks the language of the suburbs but makes some poetry with it.

Many builder houses are long and narrow, a form that minimizes construction costs because a narrow footprint allows for clear-span roof trusses and floor structure. Larum used the cost-saving strategies of this configuration along with the slope of the lot to build as much square footage as the budget would allow. The slope of the grade is steep enough to accommodate windows, so finishing the basement was a given, which meant added living space. The house he designed is essentially a 20-ft.-wide, split-level rambler with an attached garage.

This house outside of Bozeman, Montana, fits into its neighborhood of ramblers and split-levels, while distinguishing itself with enunciated overhangs, golden brackets, and a picture window made out of Kalwall.

1

The kitchen extends to encompass cabinets for food and beverage storage, while a piece of Kalwall screens off mudroom clutter. Without the screen, the first floor is one big open area of flexible space.

2

The living area is open but made cozy by variation in the ceiling height and the three large windows, which define spaces within the room.

MATERIAL WORLD

The same material that brings 26,000 sq. ft. of skylight to the Metropolitan Museum of Art in New York City stands in for the house's front window. Kalwall®, a fiberglass-reinforced face attached to a structural aluminum grid, offers insulation from the elements as well as a uniquely diffuse light. Used mostly in skylights, it can also take some load capacity, thanks to the way the metal grid is constructed. The homeowners splurged on this material for the window: A leftover piece now serves as a screen between kitchen and mudroom.

1

Think suburban, but better

The convenience of an attached garage is not to be underestimated and, echoing the nearby homes, the garage for this house is on the front. But there is no yawning mechanical door facing the street here. Instead, the garage is designed to look like part of the house. It's made more interesting with a small window that faces the street and a peaked roof. The doors are tucked away to the side.

The garage completes the T shape of the house and helps define the entryway. A picture window greets visitors at the front entrance, only this one is not glass but Kalwall. With its milky white surface and black structural grid, the window offers no views, but adds

2

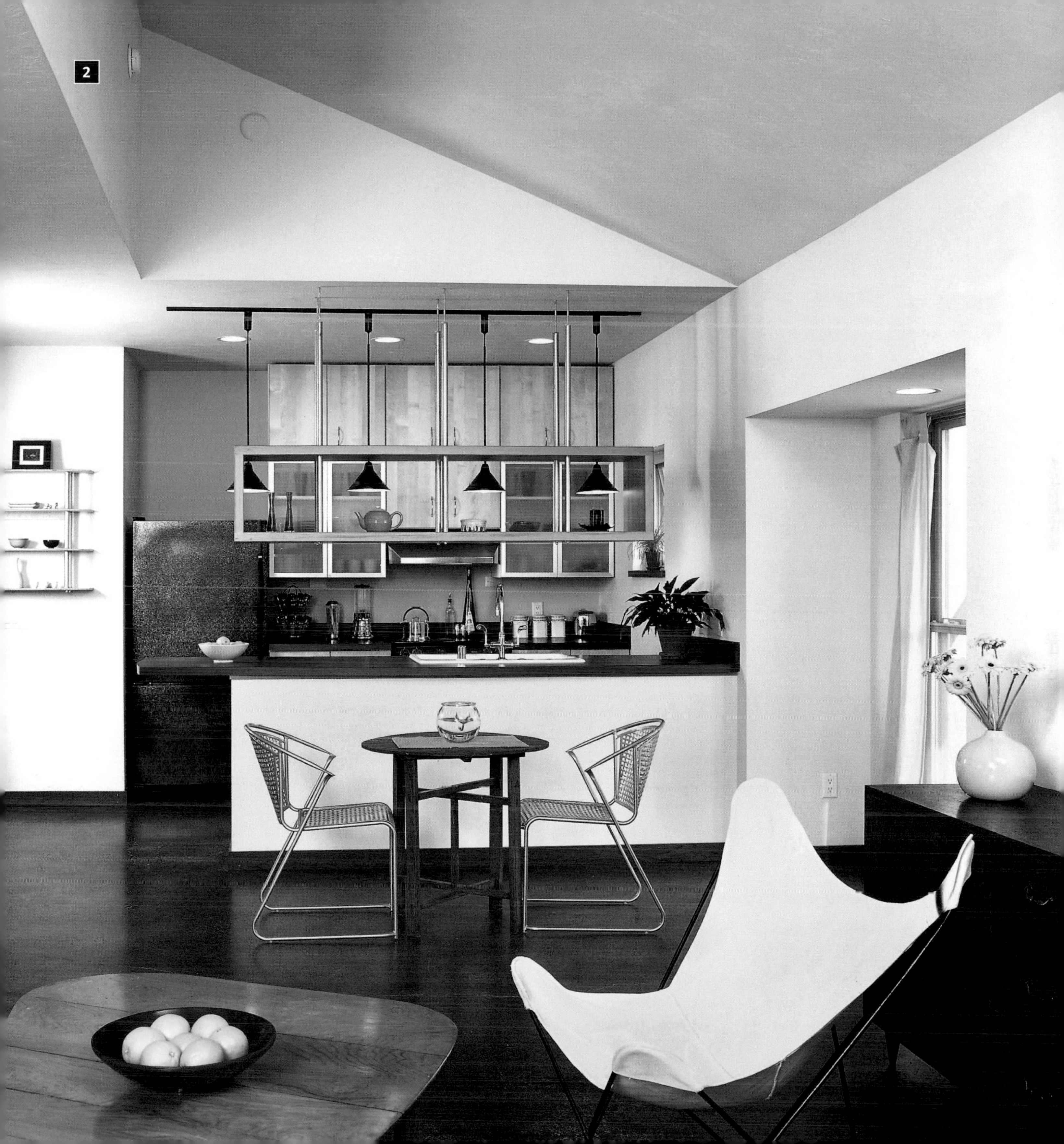

The brackets are both decorative and structural, holding up the window overhangs. The truss tails are left exposed, which creates a crafted detail in the roofline.

The garage doors are tucked off to the side; a clerestory breaks up the expanse of red wall that is the connector between house and garage. The windows are "butt-glazed," which means the two panes of glass are abutted with a sealer.

3

The interior is ruled by simplicity, with the most dramatic architecture coming from the window bays and sloped ceiling. The floors are stained concrete with a radiant heat system.

3

a geometric pattern and a warm color to the home's interior and exterior. Inside, it filters the light, while providing privacy from neighbors.

While the architect respected every building covenant in designing the exterior, he decided that the typical suburban interior, with its emphasis on rooms as opposed to spaces, would not work for the homeowners. In fact, this interior, with its poured concrete floor, looks more like a loft than a split-level ranch. Because affordable materials were used wherever possible and a few simple architectural choices were carefully made, the space is imbued with the homeowners' personal styles.

One detail transforms the modest kitchen, which features Formica countertops and IKEA maple cabinetry, into a uniquely beautiful space. A hanging shelf made from hollow-core doors and galvanized pipe provides storage and partially screens the kitchen from the rest of the living area.

1

Pocket doors, salvaged from a local high school, close off the master bedroom and nearby small changing room from the rest of the main floor.

2

This basement was designed to offer an additional 1,100 sq. ft. of space, which is presently used for offices; but the area could be converted to a family room or extra bedrooms.

Out of the Box

With risers clad in galvanized steel and treads made of walnut, the stair that leads down to the lower level looks like metal on the way up and wood on the way down. By alternating materials, the homeowners not only spent half of what a wood stair would cost, but they got two styles for the price of one—the industrial and the traditional.

2

Designing with windows

The most important design element in the house is the picture window. There are four in the living room, including the Kalwall window. The remaining three are large—10 ft. by 8 ft.—and each is set into a bay, which adds variation to the rectangular form of the house. On the exterior, each bay is connected to the roofline with a simple wooden bracket. Painted a deep golden yellow for accent, the brackets add a handmade quality to the exterior. The pattern of board-and-batten and lap-cement fiberboard provides both texture and color, which is a marked contrast to the neutral-toned, vinyl-sided homes down the street.

The house feels comfortable and warm, thanks largely to these windows. They bring in lots of sunshine, especially in the winter months when the sun is lower in the sky. In the summer months, the interior remains cool because the bracketed overhangs provide ample shade.

1

smart design, small budget

The main floor offers almost entirely flexible space and is complete with a master bedroom and bath. Laundry facilities are tucked into a closet; and a small nook, painted a cherry red, sits outside the bedroom and doubles as a changing area.

Cheap chic For finishing details, the architect looked to maximize the materials that were already in place or available off-the-shelf. An extra bit of the Kalwall was incorporated as a kind of interior window that shields the kitchen from the mudroom, which serves as an overflow, multifunction space. For trim, Larum looked al what cost the least—oak—and then discovered that walnut could be had for the same price, so he used it for baseboards, for stair treads, and to trim sills. The dark color is dramatic, rich, and lends an elegant finishing touch.

This house, which the homeowners report costs less monthly than what they used to pay in rent, has brought them home equity and a stylish, spacious, and comfortable place to live and work. In its quiet way, it also presents the seeds of a real design revolution: What if houses like this were an alternative available in all American suburbs?

Compound

In Austin's chic Zilka Park neighborhood, a reclaimed army building and a landscape design studio join forces to become a creative compound. Now owned by accomplished landscape architect Eleanor McKinney, the original house once belonged to nearby Camp Mabry. It was condemned, but, according to Eleanor, it had good bones—white oak floors and generously proportioned rooms. To fix it up, the asbestos shingles were covered with stucco and inset with wooden trim. A porch was added to create a welcoming entrance at the front. The tin roof was an inexpensive solution, and one that worked well with the simple one-story structure. Today, the house looks like a Spanish hacienda; there's a laid-back quality to it. No formality inside either—just comfortable, spare rooms with simple detailing.

After living in the house for 20 years, Eleanor recently built a 700-sq.-ft. addition, which resulted in two levels of workspace for about $50,000. Designed with architect Lars Stanley, the new landscape design studio blends almost seamlessly with the existing structure to become a place where life and work are integrated.

Marked by a rough-hewn sensibility, the addition is tucked into the back of what used to be an old army office. The porch was added to integrate the old with the new.

The home's living area shows off the simple, straightforward quality found in this reclaimed army building.

With its stucco and galvanized corrugated metal exterior, the studio addition looks like an artistic storefront. One-of-a-kind ceramic tiles were set into the stucco at the entrances. The tiles were expensive, but they were used sparingly for maximum decorative effect. Doorways were further ornamented with plant-inspired wrought-iron gates that were designed and fabricated by the architect.

The interior is ruled by the same hand-hewn feeling that informs the outside. The concrete floor, which doubles as the foundation slab, has been stained and sealed. The 2×12 pine boards from a local home center in combination with the steel angle iron make simple rustic stairs. The same wood is used to create a variegated pattern on the conference room's ceiling.

Upstairs, there's room for an office, which is filled with light. Solar panels on the studio's roof help generate power (30 percent of the energy consumed, according to Lars) and serve as a backup system in case of electrical failure. Most of the windows in the structure were found in Dumpsters and then retrofitted to open like casement windows. Lars fashioned window braces so that the new windows could be opened or locked shut. The splurge in the space was installing new clerestory windows that follow the peak of the roof.

2

The smallest decorative touches add great interest to the back entrance. A hand-made ceramic tile above the door was embedded into the stucco.

3

The French doors were added in the home's renovation to connect the dining area with the living room.

3

adding on, cutting costs

1 Eleanor's office is upstairs in the studio addition, where windows look out onto a lushly wooded backyard. Solar panels fitted to the roof generate much of the power she needs to run her office.

2 The studio's conference room is marked by a rustic simplicity, informed by the house and by the budget. Materials are reclaimed (such as the windows) or straight from the local home-improvement store.

Out of the Box

What looks like an arbor for climbing plants is also a clothesline. This unique combination of functions allows both plants and clothes to take advantage of the best sunshine in the backyard. It was a decision that took Eleanor 20 years to make: The clothesline was there originally, and she was reluctant to change what had worked for so long.

Backyard benefits

Eleanor wanted the addition to feel like its own structure, not just something attached to the house; so the studio has its own front and back doors. But at the back of the house, the two structures are tightly integrated. A few steps may have been all that was needed to reach the studio's back door, but both architect and landscape designer saw that a bit of an investment would create more outdoor living space as well. A porch now extends from the back entrance and runs the width of the house.

It's roofed with greenhouse plastic, an inexpensive material that filters light beautifully and is made to withstand the elements. Steps that run the entire length bring informal seating and create a gracious sense of connection to the patio and backyard. Here, Eleanor's gentle approach to the landscape can be appreciated. As with her own home and studio, she's created a place for inspiration.

GOOD HOUSE CHEAP HOUSE

D.I.Y.

Griz Dwight tells a story about pouring concrete countertops in his kitchen. It was late, he was out of cement, and hot water was pouring into the room from a broken valve. After shutting off the main, he made his way to his local home-improvement store, which was thankfully open at three in the morning. He was wet, covered in dust, in pain from having burned his hand, and slightly frantic. He passed a guy dressed exactly the same way, looking equally unkempt and equally unhinged. Each man picked up a bag of cement and nodded at the other in recognition.

This story is one of a few adventures Griz, an architect, and Mary Dwight had on the way to bringing back a 1930s row house in Washington, D.C. The way Griz sees it, their row house actually had little in the way of architectural character to bring back, so their renovation didn't have to be entirely respectful. But it did have to be on budget. The couple did much of the work themselves, pouring concrete countertops and hanging drywall. Completed in 2001, the 2,500-sq.-ft. home is a great example of what you can do with $30,000, if you're willing to get your hands dirty (if not scalded).

A **2,500-sq.-ft.-row house** in Washington, D.C., got a complete renovation that brought a contemporary flair to the interior. Where there were Moorish arches in the living area, now there are floor-to-ceiling openings.

The focal point of the living area is a fireplace, which was transformed from short and squat into tall and striking. Its faux finish combines a sage green with a creamy white.

One of the existing upstairs bedrooms was transformed into a shared office. The couple, both of whom work at home, shares a desk, which Griz designed and fabricated.

1

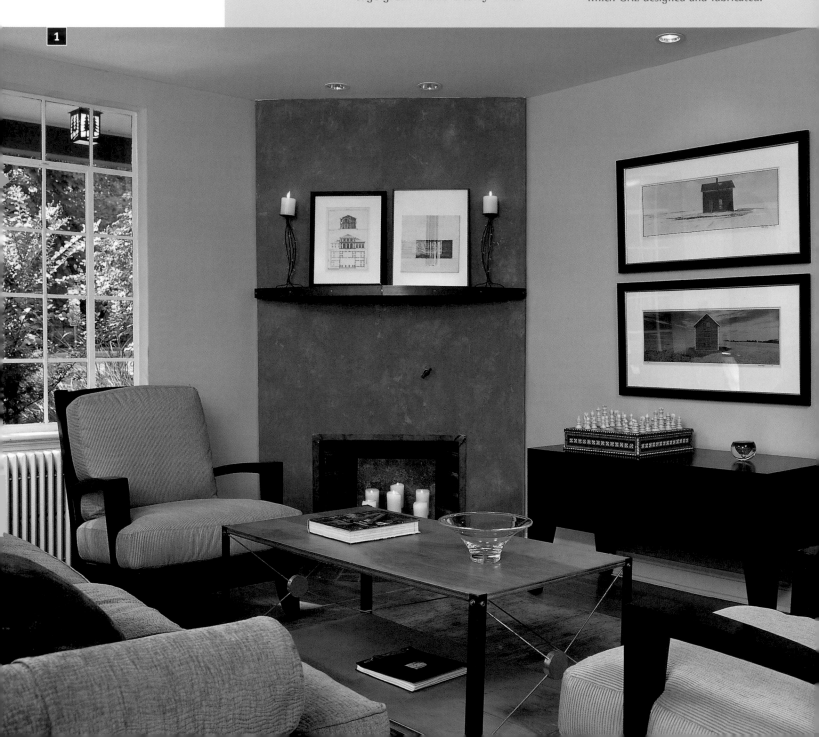

The mantel over the fireplace is made from cold-rolled steel. Most steel is hot rolled, which means that when it's red hot, it's rolled through a mill that turns it into rods or sheets or bars. Cold-rolled steel is first hot rolled and then rolled twice without heat. It's preferred for finishing details because it has a smoother surface and crisper corners, without defects or mill scale, which is what makes steel bluish.

Restoring style

The couple's limited budget forced them to carefully choose what to renovate and what to simply beautify. The row house has four levels; the two lower levels would receive a minimal fix up and remain a rental unit. The remaining floors, inhabited by the Dwights, would get the most attention. Certain projects had to be tackled: The back of the house needed structural work and every level required new windows, which would eat up some 40 percent of their funds. The kitchen was in need of a total overhaul. In fact, the entire house was close to squalor after being occupied by college students for 15 years.

The Dwights' strategy was to look at a few big changes that would add focal points to the interior spaces. The living room featured Moorish arches with low peaks. Like most row houses, there were windows on only two sides; thus the arches were actually blocking the light from streaming through the rooms. To solve this problem, the homeowners opened the arches up to the full height of the wall. The rooms now receive more light and, because the 8-ft. ceilings seem higher without the arches, the whole space feels larger.

Griz and Mary next turned their focus to a squat brick fireplace tucked into a corner of the living room. The original fireplace wasn't particularly attractive, and its scale was too small for the room. Now, the fireplace has been reinterpreted in a more contemporary style. By covering the brick with drywall, changing the mantel from varnished wood to a piece of curved, cold-rolled steel, and adding a faux finish to the wall, the fireplace is the attention-getter in the living room.

1

A formerly windowless bedroom was extended into an attached sleeping porch, which is now a light-filled sitting area enjoyed by both homeowners and pets.

2

The extensive renovation of the kitchen mingled inexpensive concrete countertops and IKEA cabinets with more expensive cork floor tiles.

ADVENTURES in Design

The homeowners poured about 64 sq. ft. of concrete countertops. While the cost in materials was about $150, Griz thinks they would have paid close to $5,000 to have the counters installed professionally. Research suggested that the hardest part of the process would be removing the forms. So Griz decided to make the forms integral to the countertops. He used more finished-looking cold-rolled steel with steel deck screws to hold the framework in place. Once the countertops were finished, you'd never guess that the steel was ever meant to be taken off.

1

Classic contemporary
While these changes were primarily cosmetic, the kitchen needed much more than a makeover. The existing kitchen was virtually postage-stamp size. By removing a wall, an attached sleeping porch on the back of the house became part of the kitchen. Now almost twice its original size, the space has the same combination of simple style and contemporary flair that is seen throughout the house. Filled with light, it features cork floors (a splurge made possible thanks to those handmade countertops).

For what many people spend on a kitchen alone, the Dwights have transformed an entire home. The renovation has increased the resale value of their house considerably, which is nothing in comparison to how their daily lives have been improved. Their house is not only an investment in their future but it's that rare gift—an expression of who they are now.

2

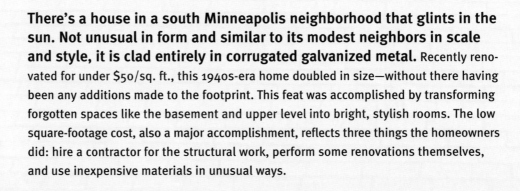

Galvanized

There's a house in a south Minneapolis neighborhood that glints in the sun. Not unusual in form and similar to its modest neighbors in scale and style, it is clad entirely in corrugated galvanized metal. Recently renovated for under $50/sq. ft., this 1940s-era home doubled in size—without there having been any additions made to the footprint. This feat was accomplished by transforming forgotten spaces like the basement and upper level into bright, stylish rooms. The low square-footage cost, also a major accomplishment, reflects three things the homeowners did: hire a contractor for the structural work, perform some renovations themselves, and use inexpensive materials in unusual ways.

The face of neat and cheap: A material commonly used in agricultural buildings has brought style and substance to a formerly bland 1940s cottage.

ADVENTURES in Design

Big enough for one person, this downstairs office closet is a marvel of efficiency. The owner built the desk from plate glass and plywood; a piece of stainless steel serves as a magnet board. Large metal brackets attached to the walls make for sturdy shelving, and a hand-crafted CD case further minimizes the clutter.

Metal, metal everywhere

Kit Kerdklai makes his living delivering mail, but his passion is design. For the house he renovated with Brad Anderson, he opted to use as much metal as possible and to balance it with wood for warmth. The reason the homeowners chose metal to clad their home? Pure nostalgia. Kit grew up in Thailand, and the galvanized material, which is a frequent choice to provide inexpensive shelter, reminded him of home. His partner, Brad, spent his childhood in a rural setting in the Midwest, where the galvanized steel is a ubiquitous material in agricultural buildings.

To install the unusual cladding, contractors stripped the house's old vinyl siding off, installed rigid insulation, then attached sheets of the corrugated galvanized steel onto the frame of the house with self-sealing sheet-metal screws. The cedar trim around the windows and the wood roof shakes on the exterior offer a soft contrast in material. Any more metal might have overshadowed the home's traditional elements; more wood would have ruined the industrial chic it now displays. The balance of materials transformed this home into a New Wave cottage.

The same metal was used throughout the interior. In the living room, a gas fireplace was tucked into a corner and framed with the steel; a slab of slate was cut to become a sit-down hearth. In what used to be the basement and is now a combination game and guest room, galvanized barn doors close off a large storage area. An extra piece of the material offers a decorative touch, serving as a backdrop for a collection of old street signs. Welded steel angle iron is used for all stair railings, and diamond plate steel covers the stair treads.

Small spaces, remade

This renovation retained the original 1,086-sq.-ft. floor plan of the house, but reinvented the functions of the existing rooms. The two original downstairs bedrooms are now a media room and sitting area, with the side-by-side closets transformed into hardworking spaces. One closet is now filled with modems, stereo equipment, and compact discs, and the other has been turned into an ingenious mini home office.

1

The renovation involved replacing all the windows in the house as well as the trim. Touches such as this fireplace surround of corrugated galvanized metal connect the interior with the home's unusual cladding.

2

Galvanized metal on a barn door track conceals storage spaces in the former basement, now reinvented as a multifunction space for entertaining and guests.

Upstairs, the existing kneewalls were transformed into a long shelf for storage and display. Skylights and unexpected windows brighten up the former attic.

Every square inch in this small kitchen has been designed to maximize its design and efficiency. Stainless steel creates a shiny backsplash. Prefinished maple boards and white tongue-and-groove pine adorn the floor and ceiling.

Out of the Box

There's a basic white refrigerator hiding underneath this stainless-steel cover. The homeowners enlisted a local metal shop to fabricate the chic steel cover to slip over the existing appliance: The cost was $200, a bargain compared to the high price of a new stainless fridge.

The couple determined to make the most of the kitchen, a 9-ft. by 10-ft. space. So they splurged on Corian countertops. And they commissioned a cabinetmaker to build a versatile island, which takes up a good 4 ft. of valuable space. The island earns its keep because of its many functions, including storage for such items as linens, a steamer, and a deep-fat fryer.

Upstairs, a rabbit warren of tiny dark-paneled rooms has been replaced with a large one-room master suite that takes advantage of the roof angles. The back of the house was expanded to raise the ceiling height, which adds space if not actual square footage. Two groupings of four small skylights were installed in the place of more expensive window dormers.

The final piece of the renovation was the garage, which was also clad in metal. Now urban and chic, the two formerly bland structures have been transformed with a cheap material you see on farm buildings. Corrugated galvanized steel proves its mettle once again.

Art House

One of the first things that the owner of this home, a transplant from Washington, D.C., to Seattle, told DeForest Ogden Design Office was that she didn't like logs. The punchline is that she was building outside of Seattle on Whidbey Island, where log cabins are as common as rain in the forecast. And though her dream house would be respectful of the rustic surroundings, she wanted a contemporary and elegant home.

With the owner's relatively modest budget and the added expense of building on an island, architects John DeForest and Lydia Marshall opted to streamline space and balance inexpensive materials with more costly custom detailing. Built in 2002 for $185/sq. ft., this stylish 1,400-sq.-ft. house takes its architectural cues from the urban sensibility of its owner and the beauty of the site. Detailed throughout with inexpensive, unexpected finishes, the house, which showcases a collection of Southeast Asian textiles, is a gallery for nature and art.

This house on Whidbey Island presents an unassuming aspect. The two simple shed roofs slope down to the south, for views and exposure, then soar to provide tall wall surfaces for displaying works of textile art.

The countertops throughout the house are made from a paper and resin product called Richlite®. Since the 1960s, this material has been used for commercial cutting and baking surfaces. And in the 1990s, skateboarders discovered its smooth durable surface for their ramps. The product is made from a cellulose-based material derived from the pulping process in paper making. Mixed with resin, the pulp is then pressed and baked. Like wood, it can be cut and sanded; and it resists stains and scratches because of its hard, nonporous surface.

Dramatic reveal

While the house is undeniably sophisticated, it blends in with its wooded surroundings. Clad with Hardipanel cement siding painted gray-green, the home is nearly hidden from the street. Visitors walk the wood-mulch path from the road to a front entrance that is tucked in where two wings of the house meet.

Inside, the subtle tones of nature are replaced by drama in the front foyer, which has a soaring 14-ft. ceiling and windows that open up to the back of the property. Walking into the foyer is a little like discovering the inside of a nautilus shell, and there's a sense of beauty in an unexpected place. The space has become a small gallery, where the owner displays a large tapestry and her collection of glass canes.

A room for everything

The owner's move to Whidbey Island came after a few years of running a textile gallery in Seattle. She needed her new house to be a place where she could both display and store her many pieces. The architects looked for ways to make every space count. As a result, the main room of the house is a detailed, adaptable space, which in its many configurations can include living, dining, kitchen, and gallery—but not all at the same time. A series of sliding plywood doors transforms the space: The doors can close off the entire kitchen from view, and the dining room table turns into a workspace where she can lay out textiles.

This main room also features built-in, custom-made drawers that store most of her textile collection. Not just functional, the drawers add a modern and gracious pattern to the room. The majority are clad in maple plywood,

1

Three plywood sliding doors cover the entire kitchen, which, when closed, transforms the room into gallery space. The dining room table doubles as a work area for laying out textiles.

2

In an innovative arrangement of space, this room can be configured for living, working, dining, and/or cooking.

1

The **floors**, which are stained and saw-cut concrete with radiant heat, make for a perfect transition to the deck and views of the forest beyond.

2

The **master bedroom** walls are used to display more of the homeowner's art collection. Sunlight (and moonlight) pours in through the skylight without damaging the valuable textiles.

Out of the Box

Both architects and homeowner wanted the house to be filled with surprises. For example, the short hallway from the foyer to the bedroom is a small space, but not a typical one. Among the artwork hanging on the wall are a couple of windows, which are like portals to the wooded world beyond. With their narrow, frame-like trim, they are meant to be mistaken for paintings.

with one stained a darker color; the rest are covered in stainless steel. The pattern transforms a plain bank of drawers into a modern decorative element that brings focus to the north wall of the house. Simple birch plywood cabinets float above both kitchen and textile storage; Richlite counters, a material made from resin and pressed paper pulp, provide durable workspace in each area.

The creative detail Low-cost materials are used throughout the house, a strategy that allowed for the more expensive, custom cabinetry and an interesting combination of materials. On the exterior, fiber cement siding is combined with aluminum reveals and stained wood trim. The eaves are angled, not straight, and add architectural detail to the exterior.

ADVENTURES in Design

Designing a beautiful house on a tight budget is one thing; designing a house that has to accommodate an art collection is another. The owner requested that there be a place to display one of her tapestries or textiles in each of the main spaces—the entry, the great room, and the master bedroom. Because many of the pieces are long, the ceilings had to be at least 10 ft. high. She also wanted the work to be visible from more than one area, which meant that the artwork, not windows, would claim the wall space and that the windows would need to be carefully placed to filter light.

The architects chose simple, bronze-finished aluminum windows. Because of the way the windows are arranged and framed (with narrow plywood and hemlock casings inside), they appear as if they were more costly wood-frame windows.

Strong light can damage art, so the windows are placed carefully to filter, not flood, the interior. Some are high and small; others are arranged around paintings, framing a view of the trees. The effect of the window placement is one of discovery because there are windows in unexpected places. Even the master bedroom offers a surprising window in the form of a skylight so that the homeowner can gaze at the moon while lying in bed.

This house is defined by details that are simple and elegant. For all its economy and restraint, it offers the ultimate in luxury: a place for art among the trees.

1

A deck that wraps around the home office space creates a contemplative spot for enjoying the light and watching the birds.

2

From the back, the house's simple and elegant detailing is in evidence. The pattern of aluminum reveals in the Hardipanel cladding is carefully considered, and the small windows protect the textiles from light.

Block

This house, with its tall, striking form composed with industrial materials, occupies its corner lot in a small Midwestern town like some kind of modern sentinel. Designed by Rob Wheat for his wife, Maxine, and their family, the house is built using concrete block—and not as a veneer on a stick-built frame. Attracted to the many practical features of the material, Rob designed a geometric house that showcases three different kinds of concrete block.

Completed in 2003 for $140/sq. ft. (including land), the house not only is a unique and livable place for a family of four but is built to withstand any kind of natural disaster. Because the Wheat house was constructed with a highly efficient but relatively expensive masonry technique, it will save energy over the years and better than compensate for the added construction cost.

This 2,300-sq.-ft. concrete block house is organized around a central vertical core that results in three levels of space. The living area features a vaulted butterfly ceiling that reaches two levels; bedrooms and a loft getaway are in the tallest part of the house.

There are two kinds of block in the living area: a standard gray block and a darker burnished block that surrounds the fireplace. Making the most of the space underneath windows, built-in plywood boxes offer space for seating and books.

A stair landing on the second level now functions as an overflow play space. Eventually, the couple will turn it into a small library, with bookshelves and built-in seats.

MATERIAL WORLD

The glazed blocks in the kitchen and bathroom look like ceramic tile. Used primarily in industrial buildings and schools and popular in car washes, these blocks are highly durable and easy to clean. They are actually structural; the glaze is applied to the face of the block. The most expensive kind of concrete block, the Wheats chose them because they reflect the integrity of the house's masonry building method.

1

Warmth without wood
It's surprising how warm and natural the interior of the house feels—as if it were filled with hardwood and trim. In fact, that look is accomplished with concrete, bamboo, and plywood. The primary block used in the house is burnished, which means it's been ground and polished. Desirable because the aggregate in the concrete makes it looks like stone, the burnished block brings a soft gray to the walls, which contrasts with the lighter gray block used in a built-in entertainment center. The soft tone is picked up by concrete floors in the entrance and kitchen.

The living area has bamboo flooring, which looks like hardwood but is a renewable resource and costs considerably less. The ceiling in the living room is dramatic: The vaulted butterfly is covered with sheet plywood, usually used as exterior cladding. Here it's

2

1

The structural steel beams that surround the windows in the dining nook create an industrial detail in the kitchen. The table was made from a leftover piece of granite used on the countertops.

2

Exposed beams intersect with the corrugated metal ceiling in the kitchen. The beams are Parallam®, a composite wood product made from long strips of wood fiber.

1

ADVENTURES in Design

The Wheats liked a corner lot in town, but the house on it was beyond repair. The couple bought it anyway, then contacted their local fire department to use the house for a controlled burn, which saves money in hauling away debris. And in some instances, the house's foundation can be saved. After some asbestos was removed, the fire department went to work. They set the place on fire several times so firemen could practice extinguishing the flames. This process was repeated until the house was structurally unsound and then the fire was allowed to finish its work.

stained dark and looks like rough fir planks. Maple plywood, with a darker finish, was used for built-in shelves that can double as seating. While the look may be of a costlier warm and woodsy interior, it's accomplished with a variety of inexpensive materials.

Eclectic touches

The juxtaposition of these materials with more expensive choices marks the kitchen, which features both plastic laminate and granite countertops. The kitchen ceiling is corrugated galvanized metal; it contrasts with custom maple cabinets, which were designed to display Maxine's extensive collection of cookie jars.

The only hardwood in the house is the fir used on the stairway. Fir is a durable hardwood with a honey color; and this touch of grain and texture goes a long way. The stairwell is positioned so that it can be seen from almost every room in the house—and because it sits in the front of the house in a sculptural glass bay, it's something of an exposed spine that is visible at night through the front windows.

Monroe, Wisconsin, the self-proclaimed cheese capital of the Midwest, might seem like an unlikely spot for this kind of house, but Rob is designing other distinctively modern homes for his neighbors. The town has put the Wheat house on the map, as another point of pride—along with the local cheddar.

Dogtrot

There's tradition at work in this casual yet sculptural Mississippi house designed for Allan and Nancy Bissinger. You see it in the elements—the way the screen porch sits on the land, in how the breezy dogtrot cuts through the middle of the house, and in the way the shed roof gently slopes upward. Although there are no columns, the steps that lead up to the deck are reminiscent of a plantation veranda. It's a southern house, only reinterpreted.

The Bissingers, who live in New Orleans, wanted a small house that they could use as a year-round getaway. Designed by Mac Ball and Catherine Smith and built in 2003, the low-slung contemporary was completed for about $145/sq. ft. It's not a fancy home, but it meets all the requirements for comfort, regardless of the temperature. The architects designed a house where dogtrot, porch, chimney, and steps are all in service to creating spaces that withstand the heat and embrace the outdoor seasons.

The dogtrot is designed for indoor–outdoor living. The steps, which connect the structure with the landscape, double as casual seating, while behind the closed barn doors is a sink, convenient for entertaining.

A screen porch is a necessity in Mississippi, and this one, which is sited for views of a small pond, functions as another room in the house.

Entirely paneled in knotty pine and efficiently laid out with areas for living, cooking, and sleeping, the spacious room looks like a cabin.

ADVENTURES in Design

In this house, the forms are beautifully composed. For example, the chimney, made from a brick fired in this area of Mississippi since 1820, sits dead center on one side of the dogtrot and adds a vertical thrust to the wedge shape. The fireplace adds a fair amount of romance, too, evoking cool nights in front of an outdoor fire. Two-sided, it warms both the interior of the dogtrot and a deck off the back.

Modern vernacular

The surrounding topography is rolling, lush land with thick primeval-looking groves of trees. Nearby, farm buildings and plantation houses sit, so it was important to design a home in keeping with its locale. The shed roof that crowns the house's wedge form is covered in metal like a barn. It rises 20 ft. and adds enough space to the living area for a sleeping loft. The angle of the roof gives the house a sculptural form that is further accentuated by the dogtrot, which divides the house in half.

The dogtrot, a popular cabin feature in the piney woods area of Louisiana, was devised to circulate air throughout the interior and continued to be prevalent in the bayou well into the twentieth century. This particular dogtrot doesn't serve as the home's only source of ventilation. Rather, it's an outdoor room that can be used

In addition to a sleeping loft tucked high over the living and dining area, this window seat carves out an intimate space in what is essentially a tall cabin of a home.

Out of the Box

The metal stair that leads up to the sleeping loft was invented by the same man who created the shrimp-peeling machine. Its alternating risers save space, and the red metal is a completing detail that brings some pizzazz to the room. Unlike wooden loft ladders, today the style is used primarily in factories.

porch with the rest of the home. From the inside, there are lovely views of the lush Mississippi surroundings. In most seasons, the screen porch functions as another outdoor room.

Cozy cabin inside

Allan wanted the house to include a fancy garage—an air-conditioned space where he could tinker. Half of the house is dedicated to that. The living area is relatively small at 600 sq. ft. and is covered in knotty pine, a big splurge compared to what drywall would have cost. But for Nancy, the wood paneling evokes fond memories of her grandparents' cabin in Alabama. The open layout here is also as cozy as that older cabin: The kitchen is tucked under the sleeping loft, which is reached by ladder.

While this house could be built anywhere in the country, there's something that is uniquely southern about it, even without porticoes and columns. There's an adventuresome design at work here that plays off both the geography and the history of its place.

year round, with a bar area and kitchen in adjacent space. The Bissingers enjoy the dogtrot so much that it has become their favorite place to entertain. Like a typical dogtrot, it can be closed off from the rest of the house by a set of doors for protection from the elements.

The porch is the third feature inspired by southern tradition. It's painted red, and on the outside it embraces a large, square window and encompasses a good portion of the house. That window isn't part of the porch, though. It belongs to the house and, from the outside, acts as a visual trick that integrates the small

Pad

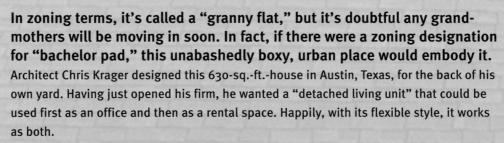

In zoning terms, it's called a "granny flat," but it's doubtful any grand-mothers will be moving in soon. In fact, if there were a zoning designation for "bachelor pad," this unabashedly boxy, urban place would embody it.
Architect Chris Krager designed this 630-sq.-ft.-house in Austin, Texas, for the back of his own yard. Having just opened his firm, he wanted a "detached living unit" that could be used first as an office and then as a rental space. Happily, with its flexible style, it works as both.

The house is designed to make the most of a trio of inexpensive materials—concrete block, tongue-and-groove pine, and glass. Each is employed in a slightly unusual way, and it's this alteration to the expected that makes the house unique. The concrete and glass give it a decidedly urban flair, while the wood makes for a haven amid the surround-ing trees. Each material also helped keep costs down: The structure was completed in 2002 for $100/sq. ft. (or for $63,000).

The wall of glass in this Austin bachelor pad opens up the modest interior to views of a tall pecan tree. Thanks to a wall of concrete block, a house on the same lot is barely visible.

1

The **bathroom** features a wall of glass mosaic tiles—a splurge that does a lot to bring style to a stripped-down room. The tiny windows let in light and binocular-like views of the yard.

2

The **living area** is the perfect hang out, with its 16-ft. ceilings and expanses of concrete and glass. A sandblasted acrylic door hides the bathroom, and upstairs more acrylic forms a balcony and bookshelf.

ADVENTURES in Design

The house has three kinds of walls: concrete, glass, and traditional stick framing clad with cement fiberboard. Each wall brings its own aesthetic and particular function. The concrete provides privacy from another house located on the same lot; the glass opens up the interior to the backyard; and the stick-frame wall houses the kitchen and bathroom, which don't need sun or soaring spaces. This was a decision that also saved some money, because it was easier to install the plumbing and mechanicals in a traditionally built wall than it would have been in a masonry wall.

Designed for privacy

There's something vaguely fortress-like about the house. In a no-nonsense way, it protects its occupants from noise and the outside world with two exterior walls made of standard, light gray concrete block.

The block walls were insulated with foam in their interiors and then stacked vertically with mortar. The few window openings in these walls are eccentric: They're small and high or door size, and they puncture the outside of the building, breaking up the expanse of gray. Inside, the block creates a modern aesthetic, which is reinforced by high ceilings and vast wall expanses.

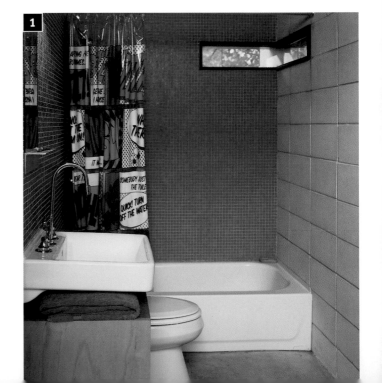

creativity and constraint

1

Upstairs, the sleeping-space loft is wrapped with tongue-and-groove pine. The wood adds warmth and coziness to create a retreat from the wide-open spaces below.

Out of the Box

The most beautiful tree on the lot was located exactly where the edge of the roof of the house would go. Cutting the tree down wasn't an option—it's an old pecan, and its canopy shades much of the backyard. So in an unconventional move, the architect designed the house with a square notched out of the roofline to accommodate the tree.

spaces. In finishing the kitchen, the architect opted for inexpensive stock materials; the bathroom is similarly stripped down. In it, concrete is made livelier with a splash of glass mosaic tile. The two rooms share a sandblasted acrylic door, which slides across the kitchen or can be pulled across the bathroom for privacy. To create a connection with the space above, the same semi-translucent acrylic is used in the sleeping loft's balcony, which also functions as a bookshelf.

Plain pine

Upstairs, the sleeping loft floor, walls, and ceiling—is finished with tongue-and-groove pine. While pine makes the interior space feel cozy, the wood also covers the exterior soffits, creating a visual bridge between the ceiling inside and the roof outside. It's as if the wood-cladding reaches right through the glass.

The house functions better as a place to live than it does as an office, reports the architect, whose firm outgrew the space in less than a year. Occupied now by a singer-songwriter who is popular in Japan, the house has found its proper incarnation as bachelor pad. Up in the wood-clad bedroom, there's a bird's-eye view of the treetops through the glass and the urban canyon of glass and concrete below.

Even though the concrete walls create lots of privacy, the home still receives plenty of light, because the north wall of the house is entirely glass. To avoid the look of an office building, the glass is angled, which brings depth to the curtain wall. Sliding glass doors open to a patio, and the glass above is two vertical sheets separated by a mullion in the center. A simple effect, angling the glass also saved money, because the glass didn't need to be structural. The upper and lower sections meet in the middle at a steel midspan brace.

If the effect of the glass and concrete walls in combination with the 16-ft. ceiling is dramatic, the tone the rest of the house sets is much more low key. Kitchen and bath are tucked under the sleeping loft, creating a stacked living function that brings more nest-like

GOOD HOUSE CHEAP HOUSE

Structure

Architect Rick Kazebee loves the skeletal outlines of a just-framed house: He sees it as a kind of receptacle for potential. Caught in that moment before insulation or cladding is applied, the structure of even the most generic home expresses the possibility for both beauty and a new life. When it came to creating his own house, it occurred to Rick that the exposed framing and structure he finds so fascinating could actually become a design element.

And so, while the front of his house looks traditional with its gable roof, the back is strikingly different. It's on that trip from front door to back that the house virtually lightens up, exposing its framing and floor plan. In the back, one sees a modern composition of wood and glass. This dichotomy between traditional and open cross section expresses something profound about the notion of home: that it can be both a sanctuary and a place for a journey.

As in a cross section, this house shows off both its structure and its organization through an artful wall of glass. The roof on the back porch is a translucent corrugated plastic that contributes to the "unfinished" look of the house.

1

The glass wall would have been prohibitively expensive if it were created using windows. Some operable ones were purchased off the shelf, but the other 125 fixed panes of glass were constructed by the homeowner with weather-stripping and wood.

2

The pine planks that cover the floor are typically used on the exterior; here they've been sealed with a heavy polyurethane coating. The stair features Simpson Strong-Ties® and plywood, which is finished with veneer on both sides.

3

The book shelves are suspended directly from the roof trusses and further supported by corner bracing. Integral to the shelving system is a pole that guides the rolling library ladder.

Completed in 2003, this Charlotte, North Carolina, house was built over the course of 4 years by Rick and his wife, Kris, who poured every amount of spare time into its completion and moved in at the first possible moment so they could build after hours. Rick understands the basics about construction, but he hired experts to take on the mechanical, electrical, and plumbing tasks. Even so, this 1,728-sq.-ft. house was built for just $50,000.

Structure exposed
With such a shoestring budget, the place to start was with a design that would be easy to build. A simple 24-ft. by 48-ft. rectangle was divided into two cubes: one where the bedrooms are stacked; the other, open to the ceiling, for living room, dining room, and kitchen. Within this straightforward framework, Rick created a consistent design vocabulary for the house; wherever possible, the structure of the elements is expressed, not covered up.

1

From the front of the house, the trusswork inside is visible through a clerestory set under the eaves. Making the journey through the house, visitors see more and more of this skeletal roof framework, which, at the back, meets a two-story wall of wood and glass. A view to the backyard reveals the beauty of the seemingly unfinished house, as the framework continues outside to form a back porch, then a simple fence.

Light from the glass wall floods the public areas, while the bedrooms and other private spaces have lower ceilings, making them cozier. A stairway that combines wood planks, birch plywood, and structural steel ties leads to a home office and master bedroom and bath. In the master bedroom, the framing members add decorative detail and somehow the whole room feels like a piece of furniture.

1

Upholstery-covered homosote panels serve as sound dampeners, and add vivid color and pattern to the public areas. They were made by the homeowners from leftover bulletin boards.

2

Because of the irregularity between the trusses, the owner installed trim to cover the edges, which creates a cabinetry-like effect that is repeated in the birch plywood wall trim.

MATERIAL WORLD

The skylight, which runs the length of the house, is an insulated acrylic and aluminum frame unit manufactured by Natural Light. The Kazebees, concerned about leaks, paid to have it professionally installed. A fairly standard ridge skylight, it was manufactured to the specified width and pitch of the house. It sets up on a 2x2 curb and has a double layer of flashing under it.

Beauty revealed Throughout, inexpensive materials such as birch plywood and stained medium-density fiberboard (MDF) are used to create a warm, natural palette. Whenever possible, the connection, the structure, or the material was left exposed for what it is. This approach to details, integral to the home's design, also had a practical aspect: Rick knew that his finishing skills were limited and that this approach would be easier for him to build. For kitchen cupboards, the homeowners considered functionality first; they needed to hide the contents from sight. With their metal screens and simple pine frames, the finished cabinets look handmade.

1

The bathroom mirror is made from construction scraps and is designed to look like the TV stand in the bedroom. A piece of leftover corrugated fiberglass over a standard row of bulbs becomes a striking light fixture.

2

The triangular-shaped clerestory adorns the front of the house and brings light into the master bedroom. The built-in unit for the television is made from construction scraps and corner brackets, which hold it to the prefab roof truss.

ADVENTURES in Design

In such a highly composed space as the master bedroom, traditional closets would have seemed out of place. So the bedroom features a dressing room, fashioned out of freestanding plywood walls. The walls are nailed to framing that is attached directly to the roof truss. Closet doors are also made from plywood and hold shelves and rods for clothing storage.

1

1

So, too, with built-in bookshelves: The shelves were hung on 1×2s, which are screwed to the wall and extend to the roof trusses. The exposed structural ties on the stairs add raw detail; even the woodstove's pipe, without a chimney on the back porch, looks like a shining tower that pierces the translucent porch roof.

The experience of living in the house is like a journey, from closed to open, from private to public, and from traditional to the sense of beauty and potential that Rick finds in structural framework. Designed to offer escape in addition to shelter, this house is much more than the sum of its parts. It transforms order, composition, and structure into an artful and meaningful architecture.

2

Farmhouse

Glen and Lisa Worley refer to the home that Lars Stanley designed for them in Elgin, Texas, as the "Ur House" because it manages to look familiar to everyone who visits. If you're versed in Americana, you might insist the house is straight out of an Andrew Wyeth painting, because of the way it so graciously sits on a sweeping field. Its wide overhangs look Chinese to visitors from China, its porch columns look French to people who know about French country houses, and to the Texas locals those very same elements make it look like a farmhouse from a past era.

With its metal-hipped roof and gracious wraparound porch, this Texas farmhouse also makes everyone who visits feel at home. During a recent home tour, the Worleys were surprised to find the whole group seated on their back porch, enjoying the view of the pond. Such comfort comes from design, not from any luxury appointments. In fact, this house was built for $80/sq. ft. in the mid-1990s.

To keep to the tight budget, the architect and builder carefully chose inexpensive but long-lasting materials. The spaces were well considered and finished simply. The combination of inexpensive materials with such a strong design resulted in a house that is extraordinarily gracious.

With its gracious details, this house speaks the vernacular language of the Texas farmhouse. It is a style that has been reinterpreted, not merely copied, with carefully considered design and materials.

1

Opting for **comfort** over quantity, the Worleys chose two larger bed-rooms instead of three smaller ones.

2

Not all kitchens need cost as much as a luxury car. From the floor to the countertops to the cabinets, everything in this crisp, country kitchen is stock or commercial grade.

Out of the Box

Architect Lars Stanley draws his blueprints by hand and he thinks he must have taken a coffee break when rendering the stairway. Builder Gordon Dietz studied the plan, carefully followed its dimensions, and built this niche in the stairway. The homeowners were initially mystified by what looked like a mistake, then determined it made a perfect spot to display shells and rocks.

Simple comfort
The idea for a farmhouse came from the architect. And the Worleys determined to put their resources into ensuring that the house would be built for the future, rather than just looking expensive, with high-end finishes.

For one, the pier-and-beam foundation was much more expensive than pouring a concrete slab, which shifts on heavy clay and can create structural problems later. A foundation that lifted the house off the ground, like the one the Worleys had built, ensured that the structure would be stable. Also, the crawl space for pipes and ducts, which can be well insulated, results in savings of at least 20 percent a year in energy costs.

Visually, the foundation is like a plinth on which the house sits, giving it stature. Otherwise, the farmhouse details on the exterior are relatively inexpensive: Instead of the quintessential wide clapboards, the exterior was clad in Hardiplank. Wood was used sparingly on the porch, and the lumber was either raw cut, which is less expensive, or stripped of bark and treated with oil.

1

1 **To make the house** feel spacious, the interior doors are glass and the room features windows on all sides, creating an enviable spot where one can actually watch the sun set and the moon rise at the same time.

2 **Though the house** is relatively new, its connections to the local history are real. A hitching post out front recalls the time when the site was a stagecoach stop.

MATERIAL WORLD

The Worleys had originally envisioned using telephone poles for porch posts, but builder Gordon Dietz happened on just-cut post oak trees at a local sawmill. Gordon thought the material was appropriate to the house because oak grows in such abundance in the area. When the posts arrived, they looked like firewood, but Gordon stripped and oiled each one on site. Leaving the natural form of the wood gives an organic and hand-built quality to the porch.

Inside, the same consideration was paid to creating spaces that would endure. The plan is open, with private spots leading into one central public room. Rather than a series of small, neglected spaces, the homeowners opted to make the rooms a comfortable size. Instead of having three small bedrooms, the Worleys decided on a spacious master bedroom and a guest room, which could accommodate visiting family. The upstairs level was conceived of as a music room for Glen, who has a collection of electric guitars, but it can double as a second guest room, as well.

A touch of grace The interior finish materials are traditional and affordable (many are commercial grade); but within the farmhouse context, these materials, which might look bland in any other setting, look charming and country. Vinyl tile you might find in a restaurant covers the kitchen, mudroom, and bathroom floors. It's not only fairly inexpensive but durable and resistant to cracking. The large speckled gray-and-white tile highlights the crisp white trim and walls. Pecan wood flooring, a local material (and so relatively less expensive than other hardwoods), is used in the common areas. The variegated wood grain also adds to the home's country feel.

The couple chose to do without certain appliances, such as a dishwasher (the Worleys enjoy washing and drying together), and to look for lower-priced fixtures. The bathrooms feature reclaimed sinks, well-made fiberglass showers, and standard fixtures. The old-fashioned light fixtures all come from flea markets and antique stores, hundreds of dollars cheaper than new ones would cost.

As the final touch, the couple had a bronze plaque made to commemorate both the architect and the builder who worked together on the house. The plaque dubs it "Hogeye Hill," which hearkens back to when the site was a stagecoach stop. And although there's nothing historic about the house, this one is designed and built to stand the test of time.

Cottage

Nestled into the pines, this house looks like it's straight out of a storybook. But the tale it might tell is more cheerful than one from the Brothers Grimm.
The house could well be a traditional New England Cape, it's so familiar in form. But clearly someone's had fun with the design. The roof is steeply pitched and the form rectangular, the overhangs are wide and the clerestory makes it seem as if the top of the house were floating.

The house was designed by architects Tamara Roy and B. K. Boley for Tamara's mother, Cheryl Simard, who wanted a residence that would take her through the next phase of her life. Cheryl had spent summers in the New Hampshire lake country: She had just remarried, had started a new job, and the kids had finally left the nest. Tamara and B. K. were just graduated from architecture school, and this was their first commission, so they were eager to realize some of their fresh ideas.

Completed in the early 1990s for $85,000, the house is small at 1,200 sq. ft.; the price reflects the streamlined square footage and the fact that both architects were involved in most every aspect of the job, from finding cheap prices on materials to wiring the house.

This cottage in the woods has a sculptural yet storybook presence, with its exaggerated roofline and extra wide cladding. Located in New Hampshire lake country, it's a whimsical year-round home.

ADVENTURES in Design

The house's floor plan makes it energy efficient. The north side is armed with what is called the "backpack." This cavity of space helps insulate the house from the cold north winds. It also features a wall of built-in storage, which is used for coats and as a pantry. The stairs, also on the north wall, further insulate the living area, as does the glass block.

1

New cape

The playful union of a modern aesthetic with a traditional form is seen throughout the house. Like a typical Cape, the roof is peaked and the cladding is wood. But the steep pitch of the roof seems almost an exaggeration, and the cladding is 2-ft. by 8-ft. sheets of marine-grade mahogany plywood set with strips of copper-anodized aluminum roof seams. Fixed glass set just beneath the eaves is an entirely modern feature, creating the illusion of a floating roof.

One way to build a house with this kind of detail on a budget is to keep it small and essentially rectangular. The first level, just 640 sq. ft., is devoted to living room, kitchen, and dining area. The space, southern in orientation, is awash in sunlight from a wall of windows. The roof overhangs are wide to provide shade in the summer months and take full advantage of limited sun during the winter.

1

The modestly sized kitchen features a warm palette, including a slate tile floor and richly figured cherry cabinets.

2

The first floor is an open room with a woodstove at one end and the kitchen at the other. The window that frames the stove not only provides views but makes the room seem larger by bringing the outdoors in.

2

1 The triangular bump-out on the front of the house is roofed with a nonoxidizing aluminum that contains copper shavings in a chemical base. It looks like copper, but won't age to a green patina.

2 The bathroom vanity is tucked into the peak of the triangle at the front of the house. The mirror reflects the triangular niche in the bedroom.

MATERIAL WORLD

Marine-grade plywood is typically used on boats. A high-quality product, it's manufactured to withstand the elements. Before installing it on the exterior of this house, the architects tested its strength by boiling it for 5 hours. While the control piece of regular plywood turned to oatmeal, the marine-grade plywood turned black but kept its form.

The second level feels like an attic loft—it's essentially an open room with a steeply angled ceiling created by the roof. Treating the space this way reduced the number of walls and the amount of insulation needed, so Cheryl was able to stay on budget. The triangular bump-out that enlivens the front facade of the house provided just enough space for the bathroom.

Glass for sky The upstairs feels like a serene nest among the trees because of its unique clerestory. This glass set under the fascia boards has the effect of bringing the treetops right into the room. Skylights, installed in the bedroom and bath for ventilation, further extend the views to the outdoors while keeping the place cool.

The roof peak transforms the bathroom into a distinctive space. The sink and vanity are inset into a triangular niche that's topped with glass. Finished simply and elegantly with standard white tile and Formica rolled into a bullnose edge, the bathroom features a Jacuzzi® tub, a splurge that completes the sense of retreat.

The blithe, peaceful presence of this home has everything to do with its simple form and a few unusual and beautiful details. Essentially two rooms, the house could have been, for the same budget, a log cabin. In the hands of young, talented architects, the traditions of New England have been reinterpreted to create a shelter with a fresh design.

Starting Modular

Carol Wilson's house could not look less like a double-wide, but it was built using manufactured housing technology for trailer-home prices. Located outside of Portland, Maine, the Scandinavian-style abode was built for $38/sq. ft. in 1992 using modular methods with upgraded materials and design innovations. Today, Carol estimates she would pay close to $68/sq. ft. for the peaked ceilings, parquet wood floors, and whitewashed pine structural beams that enliven the spacious rooms. Adding to the open feel are oversize windows that extend views outside to the wooded site.

In the early 1990s, Carol, an architect, started designing a new home: It was long and narrow, with a linear plan. Simultaneously, Susan Ruch, long involved in Portland's historic preservation movement, began to explore the production of well-designed factory-built affordable housing. The two women met, and both realized that Carol's new design might be adapted to meet the guidelines of a manufactured home that was supported by a permanent foundation but built inexpensively. They constructed the prototype, and then the architect moved in. Over the years, she has invested in it, adding a library, a studio for her architecture practice, and a sleek and modern kitchen.

The overhanging roof of the studio works to compose the entrance to the home as well. Set back just beyond the gated screen, the house is further connected by a wooden footbridge.

1

The new kitchen blends well with the Scandinavian feel of the house. Its clean, white surfaces and modern appliances are a splurge that works well with the surrounding less-expensive finish details.

2

There are many subtle design tricks in this house that work to make it feel expensive. The peak in the roof, angled at 90°, makes the ceiling soar above 8-ft. walls that are braced with delicate rafters.

MATERIAL WORLD

Standard-size windows and doors are used effectively throughout the house. In the master bedroom, a square roof window is a well-considered detail that transforms the peaked ceiling. Matched with a 6-ft. by 6-ft. sliding door, the punch-out above serves to create a sense of destination at one end of the house. The sliding door is mounted 8 in. off the floor, an unusual position that allows it to function both as a door and as a window that brings in views of trees.

1

Quality and cost Back in the planning stage, the basics came quickly—based on the dimensions of what an assembly line could build, what a truck could deliver, and what a crane could lift. Because the house is one room wide, every space benefits from two directions of light. The 72-ft. length, typical in manufactured houses, was divided in half to create two modules that could be placed at an angle. This simple adjustment creates a welcoming entryway, which was missing from most modular homes. One section holds living space and kitchen, the other bedrooms and a bathroom. Everything is on the same level; thus, while the original part of the house is small, at just under 1,200 sq. ft., its interior spaces, with exposed rafters crossing high peaked ceilings, feel large.

The changes to the original house include the kitchen, which was just remodeled. Well designed but also quite expensive, it co-exists happily with its more modestly priced surroundings. Because the room is open to the living room area, Carol wanted the cabinets to blend into the white wall. To that end they are made from lacquered

1 The square window in the study's roof peak is the same as the window in the master bedroom. They serve to mark both ends of the house.

2 The study addition opens up to the home's southern side. The trim detail on the windows and sliding doors throughout the house are extensions of the jamb, which eliminated lots of wood, trim, and casing from the prototype.

2

ADVENTURES in Design

In 2000, Carol decided to move her small architecture firm to the house, and she designed a two-story studio for the site. Completed for $70/sq. ft., the structure, which was stick built, features the same inexpensive, high-quality materials as the house. And like the house, the exterior cladding is a plywood product that resembles vertical rough-cut pine boards. The roof slopes down to a one-story height at the front, which creates a covered walkway that welcomes visitors to both the studio and the house beyond.

plywood, without pulls or knobs. The island is massive; and because it's on tall metal feet, it appears to float above the floor, which allows the floor surface to continue, and lightens its visual load on the space. Compact European appliances were a splurge, and they fit seamlessly with the kitchen's white Corian countertops.

Throughout the rest of the house, materials were chosen for cost and quality. The exterior cladding is a plywood product that resembles vertical rough-cut pine boards. Many of the windows are sliding glass doors installed 8 in. off the floor. They function as both windows and doors to outside decks.

The flooring in the house is wood parquet tile, which is among the more inexpensive hardwood floor options, and costs about what carpet does per square foot. They are installed like vinyl tiles and come presealed, which saves on finishing costs. If the floor gets damaged, the tiles can easily be replaced.

Adding a study
Using the same inexpensive materials, Carol designed a study addition, which duplicates the modular look of the original house but was stick built. A straightforward rectangular form, the addition features lots of light and a peaked roof and is the perfect place for her books and grand piano.

A curved outdoor deck connects the new room with the wooded site. To create a diagonal, which gives the sense of long views within the house, the addition is staggered off the end of the living area.

This house is so successful in terms of marrying low-cost with high design, that it's a shame there aren't variations of it all over the country today. Unfortunately, the manufacturer of the house went out of business. Carol's subsequent decision to move into the house was, she admits, supposed to be temporary. But the clean, fresh quality of the space appealed to her; and as time passes, her love for the place grows.

Architects and Designers